Cultural Humility in Libraries

Medical Library Association Books

The Medical Library Association (MLA) publishes state-of-the-art books that enhance health care, support professional development, improve library services, and promote research throughout the world.

MLA books are dynamic resources for librarians in hospitals, medical research practice, corporate libraries, and other settings. These invaluable publications provide medical librarians, health care professionals, and patients with accurate information that can improve outcomes and save lives.

Each MLA book is directly administered from its inception by the MLA Books Panel, composed of MLA members with expertise spanning the breadth of health sciences librarianship.

2023 MLA Books Panel

Members

Heather Jett, AHIP (Chair)
Mayo Clinic Libraries

Susan Maria Harnett, AHIP (Chair Designate)
Nemours Children's Health

Laureen Patricia Cantwell
Colorado Mesa University

Jeannine Creazzo, AHIP
Robert Wood Johnson University Hospital Somerset

Amanda Haberstroh, AHIP
East Carolina University

Shanell T. Stephens
University of Maryland, Baltimore

Patricia Ulmer, AHIP
Geisinger Health

Liaisons

Tamara M. Nelson, AHIP (Board Liaison)
University of Tennessee Health Science Center

Stuart Hales (Staff Liaison)
Medical Library Association

Erinn Slanina (Publisher Liaison)
Rowman & Littlefield

About the Medical Library Association

The Medical Library Association is a global, nonprofit educational organization, with a membership of more than 400 institutions and 3,000 professionals in the health information field. Since 1898, MLA has fostered excellence in the professional practice and leadership of health sciences library and information professionals to enhance health care, education, and research throughout the world. MLA educates health information professionals, supports health information research, promotes access to the world's health sciences information, and works to ensure that the best health information is available to all.

Recently Published MLA Books

Assessing Academic Library Performance: A Handbook by Holt Zaugg

Finding Your Seat at the Table: Roles for Librarians on Institutional Regulatory Boards and Committees Edited by Susan M. Harnett and Laureen P. Cantwell

Virtual Services in the Health Sciences Library: A Handbook Edited by Amanda R. Scull

Combating Online Health Misinformation: A Professional's Guide to Helping the Public Edited by Alla Keselman, Catherine Arnott Smith, and Amanda J. Wilson

Piecing Together Systematic Reviews and Other Evidence Syntheses Edited by Margaret J. Foster and Sarah T. Jewell

Accreditation in the Health Sciences: A Handbook for Librarians Edited by Darell Schmick

Essential Leadership Skills for Health Sciences Information Professionals Edited by Janet Crum and Annabelle V. Nuñez

Building Health Sciences Library Collections: A Handbook Edited by Megan Inman and Marlena Rose

Cultural Humility in Libraries

A Call to Action and Strategies for Success

Edited by
Shannon D. Jones and Beverly Murphy

ROWMAN & LITTLEFIELD
Lanham • Boulder • New York • London

Published by Rowman & Littlefield
An imprint of The Rowman & Littlefield Publishing Group, Inc.
4501 Forbes Boulevard, Suite 200, Lanham, Maryland 20706
www.rowman.com

86-90 Paul Street, London EC2A 4NE

Selection and editorial matter © The Medical Library Association 2024
Copyright for individual chapters is held by the respective chapter authors

All rights reserved. No part of this book may be reproduced in any form or by any electronic or mechanical means, including information storage and retrieval systems, without written permission from the publisher, except by a reviewer who may quote passages in a review.

British Library Cataloguing in Publication Information Available

Library of Congress Cataloging-in-Publication Data Available

ISBN: 978-1-5381-6214-9 (cloth: alk. paper)
ISBN: 978-1-5381-6215-6 (pbk)
ISBN: 978-1-5381-6216-3 (ebook)

Contents

List of Figures		ix
Preface		xi
Acknowledgments		xv

Part I: What Is Cultural Humility?

Chapter 1:	Cultural Humility: A Historical Perspective *Kenny Garcia*	3
Chapter 2:	Cultural Competence vs. Cultural Humility?: Exploring the Differences and Similarities *Nicole A. Cooke and Renee F. Hill*	9
Chapter 3:	The Role of Cultural Humility in Health Care *Kammi Y. Sayaseng*	19
Chapter 4:	Health Literacy: Bridging the Gap *Teresa Wagner and Rachel Walden*	29

Part II: Applications in Libraries

Chapter 5:	Overview of Cultural Humility Literature and Research *Erica Brody and Stacey E. Wahl*	41
Chapter 6:	Exploring Identities to Improve Library Practice *Andrea Hayes and Tamara M. Nelson*	53
Chapter 7:	Advancing Cultural Humility in Dental Education *Irene M. Lubker and Joni Nelson*	61
Chapter 8:	Building Connections, Crucial Conversations, and Cross-Cultural Relationships *Xan Y. Goodman and Twanna Hodge*	71

Chapter 9: Securing Your Mask First: Integrating Cultural Humility into Your Leadership Practice   85
Shannon D. Jones and Beverly Murphy

Chapter 10: Professional Development for Cultural Humility   103
Tish Hayes

Part III: Voices from the Field

Chapter 11: Using Your Power(s) for Good: Thoughts on Power, Privilege, and Cultural Humility   115
Gina R. Costello

Chapter 12: Cultural Humility and Black Males in the Library   121
Conrad Pegues

Chapter 13: Beyond the Rainbow: Integrating Cultural Humility into LGBTQIA+ Health Inclusion Initiatives   129
Jane Morgan-Daniel, David G. Keddle, Jacqueline Leskovec, Brenda M. Linares, Hannah M. Schilperoort, Meredith Solomon, Brandi Tuttle, and Emily Vardell

Chapter 14: Trans Inclusivity   141
Travis L. Wagner

Chapter 15: Refugee Health   147
Kunga Denzongpa

Chapter 16: Indigenous Health and Access: Dismantling Medical Oppression through Cultural Humility   151
Kevin Miller and Celeste Perez

Chapter 17: Embracing Cultural Humility to Adjust Teaching and Reference Methods for Graduate Health Sciences Students   159
Margaret Henderson

Chapter 18: Accessibility and Disability: Moving through Space   165
Lydia Nadine Collins

Index   171
About the Editors   173
About the Contributors   175

Figures

Figure 2.1 Cooke's 2017 Cultural Competence Continuum, illustrated
by David Michael Moore   15
Figure 6.1 Definitions of Identity Types   54
Figure 6.2 Understanding Your Identity   56
Figure 8.1 Three Pillars of Cultural Humility   72

Preface

Have you heard of Charles Stratton, Millie and Christine McKoy, Joseph Merrick, Chang and Eng, Raymond Robinson, or Robert Wadlow? What do they have in common? They were all referred to as freaks at some point because they were different. However, they were not freaks but individuals whose lives were impacted by genetics, environment, and perhaps poor health. Their lived experiences often lacked compassion, empathy, and understanding, beckoning for a "sense" of cultural humility. Cultural humility is a process of self-reflection. This book discusses the "sense" of cultural humility related to awareness, consciousness, observation, perception, and recognition.

Against the backdrop of issues related to the "isms" (ableism, ageism, classism, racism, sexism, sizeism, etc.), health literacy, bias, power dynamics, and more, this book attempts to unpack the concept and convey the challenges library workers face when attempting to create culturally humble library environments for staff and patrons. How would the health disparities of the individuals mentioned previously be addressed in our communities today? Would they receive compassionate care in our health institutions and our libraries? Though this may seem exaggerated, the questions are not without merit.

As our journey began with this labor of love of working on a second book, we watched the inauguration of the forty-sixth president of the United States, Joe Biden, and vice president, Kamala Harris, the first woman, first Black person, and first Asian American elected to this role. Though we—as two Black women—were not physically present in the same room during this historic event, our minds, emotions, thoughts, and feelings shared the same space. In our first book, *Diversity and Inclusion in Libraries: A Call to Action and Strategies for Success*, we stated that "it is also critical to pay attention to social, cultural, and political factors that are affecting communities across the United States because these larger movements may be hampering diversity and retention efforts" (Jones & Murphy, 2019: 76). Once again, this new edited volume aligns with world events—the core of which is a desperate cry for self-reflection.

President Biden's speech was filled with many references to cultural humility, whether articulated in that specific sense or not. His uplifting cry for healing and a stop to an "uncivil war" was in direct response to events that occurred on January 6, 2021, when a group of domestic terrorists stormed the U.S. Capitol in a violent attack against the 117th U.S. Congress, resulting in multiple deaths, numerous injuries, and hundreds of arrests. A mob of President Donald Trump's supporters executed this insurrection in an attempt to overturn his defeat in the 2020 presidential election. As is often the case, a historical moment that should have been celebrated was overshadowed by a violent event.

Though this book explicitly addresses cultural humility in the context of libraries, we must recognize the impact of external forces that shape our observations and behavior. Unity is one of the goals of cultural humility, which beckons you to self-reflect by interrogating your assumptions, perspectives, beliefs, values, and daily actions.

The book is divided into three parts: "What Is Cultural Humility?" "Applications in Libraries," and "Voices from the Field."

Part 1 addresses what cultural humility is and the importance and relevance of its role in health care. Chapter 1 offers a historical perspective, chapter 2 discusses the differences and similarities between cultural humility and cultural competence, chapter 3 explores the role of cultural humility in health care, and chapter 4 highlights the integral role of health literacy in bridging the gap between health care and libraries.

In part 2, the authors describe how they apply principles of cultural humility in their work environments via lessons learned, practical strategies, development opportunities, and challenges when integrating cultural humility in library settings. Chapter 5 provides an overview of cultural humility literature and research; chapter 6 explores the role of identities in improving library practice; chapter 7 offers strategies for increasing humility; chapter 8 discusses the process of building connections, crucial conversations, and cross-cultural relationships; chapter 9 examines cultural humility from the leader's perspective, and chapter 10 provides an overview of professional development and training opportunities for learning more about cultural humility.

In part 3, the voices of diverse professionals unpack the application of cultural humility through their eyes, sharing their stories of what cultural humility has meant in their lives, how they have applied it in their work, and the challenges they have faced in doing so. Part 3 kicks off with chapter 11 offering insight into the intersection of power, privilege, and cultural humility, and it concludes with chapter 18, where the author discusses accessibility and disability. In between these voices, the authors address the role of cultural humility in relation to being a Black male in the library, moving beyond the rainbow with LGBTQIA+ health inclusion initiatives, trans inclusivity, refugee health, Indigenous health, and library instruction.

With today's rapidly evolving sociopolitical landscape, cultural humility is needed now more than ever. The surge in book bans, characterized by attempts to censor narratives and stifle diverse viewpoints, underscores the need to welcome, respect, honor, and embrace the unique cultures and perspectives we bring to our work in libraries. The racial awakening in 2020 magnified the deep-rooted inequities and systemic racism that continue to exist in the United States, urging individuals to engage in introspection and proactive learning to dismantle these injustices. Cultural humility provides a framework for acknowledging the oppressions faced by individuals from historically excluded communities, while encouraging ongoing self-education and empathy to enhance our understanding of the lived experiences of others. As we strive for greater inclusivity and progression of social justice in libraries, embracing cultural humility will be a powerful tool in nurturing dialogue, understanding, and positive transformation.

Much like our first book, *Cultural Humility in Libraries* is a call to action for readers to look inward to assess the role and impact of cultural humility in their own lives. In particular, readers are encouraged to deliberately reflect and think critically about how their thoughts, words, and actions impact the people around them.

REFERENCES

Jones, S. D., & Murphy, B. (2019). Recruiting and Retaining a Diverse Workforce. In *Diversity and inclusion in libraries: A call to action and strategies for success*. Rowman & Littlefield.

Acknowledgments

An African proverb says it takes a village to raise a child. This is indeed true for completing a book project. Without the support of our families and frolleagues, we could not have brought this book to completion.

We would like to thank our contributors for answering the call to participate in this project. We are grateful for your persistence and your patience. Your collaboration played an integral role in transforming our vision into the reality of what became *Cultural Humility in Libraries*. Your insights, expertise, and dedication have enriched this project, resulting in a valuable resource that promotes understanding, inclusivity, and cultural awareness within libraries. Your contributions will undoubtedly leave a lasting impact on the way libraries engage with diverse communities.

We extend heartfelt thanks to our tribe, the African American Medical Librarians Alliance (AAMLA) Caucus of the Medical Library Association, for loving, affirming, encouraging, and supporting us. We appreciate your collective effort to show up and stand in solidarity with us on important topics, especially those related to diversity, equity, inclusion, and belonging. We are so very proud to stand among you as colleagues.

Finally, we express our gratitude to our readers. We hope you enjoy reading the chapters that comprise this volume and that you find the insights shared helpful on your journey to becoming culturally humble information professionals.

Part I

What Is Cultural Humility?

1

Cultural Humility

A HISTORICAL PERSPECTIVE

Kenny Garcia

Cultural humility and cultural competency are concepts and frameworks rooted in social work, pediatrics, and public health. The concept of cultural humility was first proposed as an intervention by Tervalon and Murray-Garcia in 1998 to counter the progression and growth of cultural competence as a concept and framework developed by Gallegos in 1982 and further expanded upon by Cross, Bazron, Dennis, and Isaacs in 1989 to address interpersonal and systemic racism. Though this chapter highlights key publications, perspectives, and elements/terms for cultural competency and cultural humility, it serves as an overview, not an exhaustive list. Additionally, it outlines the development of cultural humility as a concept and framework while examining when and how it was first introduced as a counterpoint to cultural competency. Cultural competency is a set of related behaviors, attitudes, and policies that support interpersonal, agency-wide, and systemic cross-cultural work (Cross et al., 1989). It is the ability of organizations to honor and respect the beliefs, interpersonal styles, attitudes, and behaviors of their multicultural clients and staff through policy, administration, and practice (Roberts et al., 1990). In health care "cultural competence is the demonstrated awareness and integration of three population-specific issues: health-related beliefs and cultural values, disease incidence and prevalence, and treatment efficacy. But perhaps the most significant aspect of this concept is the inclusion and integration of the three areas that are usually considered separately when they are considered at all" (Lavizzo-Mourey & Mackenzie, 1996). Cultural competence also supports caring for patients with diverse values, beliefs, and behaviors by developing needs-based assessments to meet patients' social, cultural, and linguistic needs (Betancourt et al., 2002). Denboba (MCHB, 1993) states, "Striving to achieve cultural competence is a dynamic, ongoing, developmental process that requires a long-term commitment."

There are five elements related to the cultural competency framework that institutions, agencies, and systems use:

1. valuing diversity;
2. having the capacity for cultural self-assessment;
3. being conscious of the dynamics inherent when cultures interact;
4. having institutionalized cultural knowledge; and
5. having developed adaptations to service delivery reflecting an understanding of cultural diversity (Cross et al., 1989).

The National Center for Cultural Competence (1998), citing Cross et al., states the following:

- Cultural competence in organizations requires a defined set of values and principles, and those within organizations must demonstrate behaviors, attitudes, policies, and structures that enable them to work effectively cross-culturally.
- Cultural competence in organizations requires the capacity to (1) value diversity, (2) conduct self-assessment, (3) manage the dynamics of difference, (4) acquire and institutionalize cultural knowledge, and (5) adapt to diversity and the cultural contexts of communities they serve.
- The above must be incorporated in all aspects of policymaking, administration, practice, and service delivery, and must systematically involve consumers, families, and communities.
- Cultural competence is a developmental process that evolves over an extended period. Both individuals and organizations are at various levels of awareness, knowledge, and skills along the cultural competence continuum.

According to Denboba (MCHB, 1993), cultural competence requires planning and interventions at various levels of policymaking, infrastructure building, program administration and evaluation, the delivery of services and enabling supports, and the individual.

Cultural competency work can be done at the *individual level* by examining one's beliefs and values and developing values, knowledge, skills, and beliefs that enable people to work cross-culturally (Denboba-MCHB, 1993). Examples of cultural competency work at the *institutional level* (Denboba-MCHB, 1993).

- Review and revision of mission statements
- Policies and procedures
- Administrative practices
- Staff recruitment, hiring, and retention
- Professional development and in-service training
- Translation and interpretation processes
- Family/professional/community partnerships
- Health-care practices and interventions, including addressing racial/ethnic health disparities and access issues
- Health education and promotion practices/materials
- Community and state needs assessment protocols

According to Denboba (MCHB, 1993), cultural competency requires that organizations, programs, and individuals be able to:

1. value diversity and similarities among all peoples;
2. understand and effectively respond to cultural differences;
3. engage in cultural self-assessment at the individual and organizational levels;
4. make adaptations to the delivery of services and enabling support; and
5. institutionalize cultural knowledge.

As a counterpoint to cultural competency, Tervalon & Murray-Garcia proposed cultural humility as a framework. Cultural humility is an active commitment to an ongoing, lifelong learning process that fosters a more equitable relationship between physicians, patients, communities, colleagues, and peers. This process requires humility and incorporates patient-focused interviewing and care (Tervalon & Murray-Garcia, 1998).

According to Tervalon & Murray-Garcia (1998), there are four key concepts in a cultural humility framework:

1. lifelong process—requires self-reflection, inquiry, and learning;
2. self-reflection—requires an understanding of our own beliefs and cultural identities;
3. self-critique—requires a consistent self-examination with a desire to continually learn and grow, as our work is never done;
4. critical consciousness—requires an understanding of our assumptions, biases, and values.

Cultural humility has been a framework utilized by library workers in various types of libraries and settings (Cooke, 2017; Andrews & Watanabe, 2018; Hodge, 2019; Hurley et al., 2019; Epsten, 2021; Goodman & Nugent, 2020; Tai, 2021; Getgen, 2022; Hurley et al., 2022; Ilett, 2023; Pegues, 2023; Truesdale et al., 2023). This is by no means an exhaustive list of examples, but they highlight the work of LIS (library and information science) educators and students; public, academic, and health and medical librarians; and archives. This represents a significant professional shift, as seen through the recent rescinding of the ACRL Diversity Standards: Cultural Competency for Academic Libraries (2012) and the adoption of the joint ALA/ARL Cultural Proficiencies for Racial Equity Framework (2022). This marks a transformative shift toward adopting a cultural humility framework in the LIS profession.

REFERENCES

American Library Association (ALA), Association of College & Research Libraries (ACRL), Association of Research Libraries (ARL), & Public Library Association (PLA). (2022). *Cultural proficiencies for racial equity: A framework*. https://www.ala.org/pla/initiatives/edi/racialequityframework

Andrews, N., Kim, S., & Watanabe, J. (2018). Cultural humility as a transformative framework for librarians, tutors, and youth volunteers: Applying a lens of cultural responsiveness in training library staff and volunteers. *Young Adult Library Services, 16*(2), 19–22.

Association of College and Research Libraries (ACRL). (2012). *Diversity standards: Cultural competency for academic libraries.* http://www.ala.org/acrl/standards/diversity

Betancourt, J., Green, A. & Carrillo, E. (2002). *Cultural competence in health care: Emerging frameworks and practical approaches*. The Commonwealth Fund.

Cooke, N. (2017). *Information services to diverse populations: Developing culturally competent library professionals*. Libraries Unlimited, an imprint of ABC-CLIO, LLC.

Cross, T., Bazron, B., Dennis, K., & Isaacs, M. (1989). *Towards a culturally competent system of care* (vol. 1). Georgetown University Child Development Center, CASSP Technical Assistance Center.

Denboba, D., U.S. Department of Health and Human Services, Health Services and Resources Administration (1993). MCHB/DSCSHCN Guidance for Competitive Applications, Maternal and Child Health Improvement Projects for Children with Special Health Care Needs.

Epsten, J. (2021). Transformation through cultural humility: Developing an online curriculum for supporting transgender and gender variant people in libraries. [Masters paper]. https://doi.org/10.17615/4x5v-cb34

Gallegos, J. S. (1982). The ethnic competence model for social work education. *Color in a White Society*, 1–9.

Georgetown University Center for Child and Human Development (GUCCHD). (n.d.).

Getgen, C. (2022). Cultural humility in the LIS profession. *The Journal of Academic Librarianship, 48*(4), 102538. https://doi.org/10.1016/j.acalib.2022.102538

Goodman, X., & Nugent, R. L. (2020). Teaching cultural competence and cultural humility in dental medicine. *Medical Reference Services Quarterly, 39*(4), 309–322. https://doi.org/10.1080/02763869.2020.1826183

Hodge, T. (2019). Integrating cultural humility into public services librarianship. *The International Information & Library Review, 51*(3), 268–274. https://doi.org/10.1080/10572317.2019.1629070

Hurley, D. A., Kostelecky, S. R., & Townsend, L. (2022). *Cultural humility.* ALA Editions.

Hurley, D. A., Kostelecky, S. R., & Townsend, L. (2019). Cultural humility in libraries. *Reference Services Review, 47*(4), 544–555. https://doi.org/10.1108/RSR-06-2019-0042

Ilett, D. (2023). Learning to put people first: Cultural humility, funds of knowledge, and information literacy instruction with first-generation students. In M. Mallon, J. Nichols, E. Foster, A. Santiago, M. Seale, & R. Brown (eds.), *Exploring inclusive & equitable pedagogies: Creating space for all learners* (vol. 2, pp. 539–548). Association of College and Research Libraries.

Lavizzo-Mourey, R., & Mackenzie, E. (1996). Cultural competence: Essential measurement of quality for managed care organizations. *Annals of Internal Medicine, 124*(10), 919–926.

National Center for Cultural Competence (NCCC). https://nccc.georgetown.edu/

Pegues, C. (2023). Antiracism cultural humility and black males in the library. In K. Black & B. Mehra (eds.), *Antiracist library and information science: Racial justice and community* (Advances in Librarianship, Vol. 52, pp. 149–155). Emerald Publishing Limited, Bingley. https://doi.org/10.1108/S0065-283020230000052015

Portland State University. Regional Research Institute. (1988). Services to minority populations: Cultural competence continuum. *Focal Point, 3*(1), 1–4. https://archives.pdx.edu/ds/psu/34095

Roberts, R., et al. (1990). *Developing culturally competent programs for families of children with special needs* (monograph and workbook). Georgetown University Child Development Center.

Tai, J. (2021). Cultural humility as a framework for anti-oppressive archival description. In E. Arroyo-Ramírez, J. Jones, S. O'Neill, and S. Smith (eds.), Radical empathy in archival practice (Special issue). *Journal of Critical Library and Information Studies, 3*(2). DOI: 10.24242/jclis.v3i2.120

Taylor, T., et al. (1998). *Training and technical assistance manual for culturally competent services and systems: Implications for children with special health care needs.* National Center for Cultural Competence, Georgetown University Child Development Center.

Tervalon, M., & Murray-Garcia, J. (1998). Cultural humility versus cultural competence: A critical discussion in defining physician training outcomes in multicultural education. *Journal of Health Care for the Poor and Underserved, 9*(2), 117–125.

Truesdale, A., Looby, K., Lampkowski, C., & Moore, A. (2023). Conversations that matter: Engaging library employees in DEI and cultural humility reflection. *Urban Library Journal, 29*(1). https://academicworks.cuny.edu/ulj/vol29/iss1/1

2

Cultural Competence vs. Cultural Humility?

EXPLORING THE DIFFERENCES AND SIMILARITIES

Nicole A. Cooke and Renee F. Hill

The terms "cultural competence" (CC) and "cultural humility" (CH) have been used synergistically (Campinha-Bacote, 2018) and complementarily (Yancu & Farmer, 2017). While they are wholly complementary concepts and lenses through which we view the world, they are different in their nuances. However, the concepts are similar in that they both:

- emphasize valuing, promoting, and embracing diversity;
- bring about increased cultural knowledge and appreciation;
- require self-reflection and self-analysis;
- have implications, applications, and responsibilities that result in improved interactions at both the individual and organizational levels.

In recent years, some researchers and practitioners have called for moving away from emphasizing the term "cultural competence" in favor of increased understanding and usage of the term "cultural humility" (Hurley et al., 2019; Lekas et al., 2020). This is primarily because the former implies a series of steps that lead to a specific endpoint while the latter is "a life-long process of developing self-awareness, openness, respect for cultural difference and examining power imbalances" (Markey et al., 2021, 2725). But in reality, CC and CH work together to pose the classic chicken-and-egg conundrum: Which concept comes first? Which concept is better? There is a meaningful semantic difference between CC and CH and the relationship between the two concepts.

It can be argued that CC and CH need each other and, therefore, should not/cannot be separated and/or used in isolation. Cultural humility (a disposition) is needed to develop meaningful cultural competence (ongoing critical self-reflection work). And the more CC we acquire (learning and growing beyond our current capacity), the more we realize how much we still do not know (the essence of humility). This chapter examines both concepts and offers our reflections on the relationships between them.

EVOLVING TERMS; EVOLVING UNDERSTANDING

Cultural Competence

There is some debate as to what exactly we mean when we talk about cultural competence. Slightly different disciplinary manifestations exist across myriad fields that engage with the public, such as nursing (Brouse, 2007; Gillson & Cherian, 2019), psychiatry (Bell, Williamson, & Chien, 2008), occupational therapy (Matteliano & Stone, 2014), clinical psychology (Young et al., 2022), public health (D'Elia et al., 2009), child and family welfare (Lawrence et al. 2012), law enforcement (Moon, Morgan, & Sandage, 2018), education (Byrd, 2023), social work (National Association of Social Workers, 2015; Tahir, 2020), and library and information science (LIS) (Overall, 2009; Villagran & Hawamdeh, 2020). Cultural competence is also discussed in terms of outcomes—possessing the ability to interact effectively with some sort of racial, national, ethnic, or religious "other" across differences in "language, thoughts, communications, actions, customs, beliefs, values and institutions" (Centers for Disease Control and Prevention [CDC], n.d.).

Cross et al. (1989) presented CC as a continuum of attitudes and behaviors that included the following:

1. Cultural destructiveness: racism and attitudes that actively harm and/or denigrate other cultures
2. Cultural incapacity: no intent to actively harm, but racism and destructive attitudes remain
3. Cultural blindness, otherwise known as color blindness: a deliberate lumping together of groups and refusal to acknowledge differences between them
4. Cultural pre-competence: acknowledgment of the differences between groups, but little to no movement toward working with or for diverse groups
5. Basic cultural competence: increasing acceptance and respect for differences, efforts to engage in self-assessment, and research about diverse groups

6. Advanced cultural competence: high levels of respect for and knowledge of other cultures, actively working for and with diverse groups

Though Cross et al.'s cultural competence model was first conceived over thirty years ago and some of the language used is now outdated and considered culturally insensitive and ableist, the model is still useful when contemplating individual development of cultural competence as it implies progression and movement. Cooke (2017) suggested that a more helpful representation of the concept is in the form of a circle or cycle. That is, instead of a straight line and a definitive process, cultural competence is an ongoing process, with continuous movement back and forth (see Figure 2.1). Maintaining cultural competence requires constant work *and* humility, and if that work is not done, it is likely that an individual will experience prolonged periods of regression interspersed with advancement along the continuum. It is also possible to demonstrate highly developed cultural competence in one environment and not in another. Each community is distinct with its own needs and challenges. There are also communities within communities, all of which deserve their own cultural competence acquisition and maintenance process. Cultural competence is more than a simple skill set. Rather, it is a foundational knowledge base that requires us to be critical thinkers, critically conscious, and culturally humble (Kumagai and Lypson, 2009).

Whereas early discussions on inter- and cross-cultural competence often framed cultural competence as a knowledge base and standardized set of skills to be mastered, more recent considerations focus on a set of dispositions, values, and reflexive practices. For example, Overall (2009) defines cultural competence as the capacity to recognize "the significance of culture in one's own life and in the lives of others," to "know and respect diverse cultural backgrounds," and to "fully integrate the culture of diverse groups into services, work, and institutions" (Overall 2009, 189–190). This shift made sense, given the critiques of cultural competence as a fixed knowledge base that could be studied, learned, and completed. Acknowledgment of culture as dynamic and contextual prompted the question, "How can we become competent at something that is continually changing?" (Dean 2001, 625).

Cultural competence can be seen and felt on the internal, interpersonal, meso (organization), and macro (society) levels. Boyle and Springer (2008) connect cultural competence to the capacity for critical analysis, claiming that culturally competent practitioners should understand "(1) how ethnicity, social class, and oppression contribute to group identity, coping skills, and problems encountered by minority groups, (2) how group factors interact with individual development, and (3) how inequity is upheld in social service systems" (Boyle & Springer 2008, 58).

Cultural Competence in LIS

As an ideal or value, CC challenges information professionals to work purposefully and enthusiastically with and for community members of diverse backgrounds and cultures, as they are aware of the richness that exists in all cultures. More detailed and substantive than plain cultural awareness and cultural sensitivity, cultural competence compels us to *act* and not just be abreast of people's differences, and it should be a goal for individuals *and* organizations. If we consider cultural competence a value, it can facilitate this learning, which enables us to codify that value in our field.

"Many fields have codified cultural competence. It may be time for librarianship to adopt a similar code" (Press & Diggs-Hobson, 2005, 407). LIS was behind the curve when Press and Diggs-Hobson (themselves medical librarians who were aware of the cultural competence discussions in the applied health sciences) made this suggestion in 2005. These authors, along with Patricia Montiel Overall (2009), Vanessa Morris (2006), and Ghada Elturk (2003), were among the first to apply cultural competence to librarianship. Since then, cultural competence has been a consistent part of the LIS literature and conversation, including a textbook by Cooke (2017) and numerous articles (e.g., Blackburn, 2020; Cooke & Jacobs, 2018; Engseth, 2018), chapters (e.g. Kumasi & Hill, 2019), books (e.g., Overall, Nuñez, & Reyes-Escudero, 2015; Naidoo, 2014), bibliographies (e.g., Cooke & Hill, 2017), presentations, conferences, and calls to action.

In 2009, Overall warned against using cultural competence as a buzzword, which unfortunately still happens quite a bit. Cultural competence is thrown around without context, is conflated with other EDI (equity, diversity, and inclusion) terms, and has been used to allow people to check professional development boxes in order to claim enlightenment. Cultural competence is so much more than an hour-long training or workshop exercise. As Elturk (2003) explained, cultural competence necessitates continual work, commitment, and practice. There is no golden rule or one right way to achieve and maintain cultural competence; rather, it's like learning how to ride a bike and practicing again and again to attain and *maintain* agility.

Cultural Humility

Cultural humility has its own important body of research and application to community-facing service work (e.g., counseling, nursing, teaching, librarianship). In recent years there have been articles suggesting that cultural humility should supplant cultural competence (Getgen, 2022). However, like cultural competence, cultural humility is an "ongoing, courageous, and honest process of self-critique and self-awareness" that challenges information professionals to examine their "own patterns of unintentional and intentional racism, classism, and homophobia" (Tervalon & Murray-Garcia 1998, 120). Also, as an interdisciplinary concept rooted in the applied health sciences, cultural humility extends the idea that cultural competence is a way to recognize the power dynamics and imbalances that exist between service providers and those receiving services. Cultural humility asks practitioners to rectify these power imbalances, especially in regard to race, ethnicity, class, linguistic ability, and sexual orientation. Compelling us to act toward equity, cultural humility is really a social justice issue. Cultural humility is not a static end goal but a dynamic social justice orientation that culturally competent practitioners engage in when serving their diverse communities and stakeholders.

Numerous scholars have considered elements that lead to developing cultural humility (for example, Abe, 2020; Farrelly et al., 2022; Markey et al., 2021). Foronda et al. (2016) provided a concrete list of five attributes contributing to an individual's successful journey through the lifelong process of developing cultural humility:

1. Openness: The quality of being willing to explore new ideas (p. 211), this characteristic is essential in that library professionals must be sincerely interested in and open to having interactions with people from various backgrounds.
2. Self-awareness: It is impossible to course-correct, change, or grow without first being cognizant of one's "strengths, limitations, values, beliefs, behavior, and appearance to others" (p. 211). The self-aware individual can notice areas of strength and consider areas that need to be reinforced.
3. Egolessness: The very essence of demonstrating humility is the willingness and ability to discard one's ego and tendency toward self-importance. Possessing this characteristic allows the individual to view everyone as worthy, valuable, and deserving of respect regardless of actual or perceived title or social status.
4. Supportive interaction: This characteristic involves the individual engaging in positive exchanges with others.
5. Self-reflection and critique: The final attribute identified as necessary to demonstrate evolution in the process of becoming culturally humble involves deliberate, critical, and perhaps painful analysis of one's thought processes about and interactions with others (Hodge, 2019).

Although we understand the case made for replacing cultural competence with cultural humility, we see the two concepts as enmeshed and complimentary. In Cooke's 2017 version of the Cultural Competence Continuum (see Figure 2.1), cultural competence is embedded within cultural humility to emphasize the action required once cultural competence is part of an individual's regular way of being. In many ways, cultural competence and cultural humility are so intertwined it reminds one of the chicken-and-egg conundrum:

Which comes first? Which concept better informs the other? We suggest that they are both fundamentally action-based and inform each other; therefore, we need both of these concepts and lenses to accomplish the work information professionals need to do about and for diverse populations. Both CC and CH require inward-facing critical consciousness and reflection, and from this they inspire action to continuous learning about and ultimately implementing the value of different voices and perspectives.

With this in mind, and in the spirit of CH, the various and separate CC models found in LIS, education, and applied health sciences literatures (including Cross et al.'s 1998 model and Cooke's 2017 model) need to be critically questioned and updated to further infuse cultural humility and to better contextualize the complicated and multiple processes people encounter, complete, or abandon when working toward cultural competence and humility. Similarly, there are numerous CH models that also warrant examination, updating, and integration. In addition to updated language, the models need to elucidate the relationship between CC and CH more fully and approach both concepts more holistically. For example:

- There are precursors to CC and CH (including empathy, understanding privilege and oppression, etc.), and neither are without personal challenge or effort. Maintaining both over time requires a significant commitment to equity and justice.
- CC and CH can be nebulous and fluid—are categories in the model really rigid and fixed?
- How do people really move from one level of competence and humility to the next? It certainly takes more than professional reading and workshops.
- CC and CH require some psychological safety and confidence, and it is possible that everyone is not ready to embark on this journey, which can cause people to reject these concepts.
- Different people go through these processes of reflection in very different ways. How do we account for this, and for the realization that what might take one person a year to achieve might take someone else a decade? How does this impact the work to be done in the profession? Or does it really matter if people eventually reach the places they need to be?
- And then there's action. Once the internal work is done to achieve and maintain CC and CH, what comes next? What is the ultimate point of CC and CH? Where do they lead?

Ideally, they lead to action and justice. The models and discussions about CC and CH need to be much more nuanced to reflect the true nature of the humans participating in these experiences.

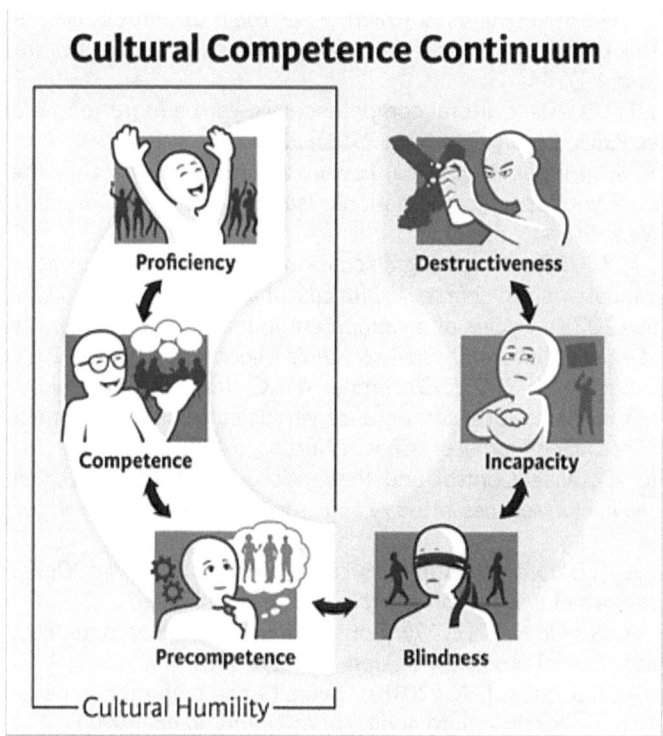

Figure 2.1. Cooke's 2017 Cultural Competence Continuum.
Nicole Cooke/David Michael Moore (Illustrator)

CONCLUSION

Striving for cultural humility results in individuals gaining "mutual empowerment, respect, partnerships ... and lifelong learning" (Foronda et al., 2016, 213). Ultimately, cultural competence and cultural humility need *not* be viewed as either/or propositions, where one must be discarded in favor of the other. Instead, they are powerfully and inextricably interwoven, allowing LIS professionals to strive for competence in interactions where multiple cultures are represented and consistently demonstrate dedication to the process of being humble and celebrating themselves and others (Figure 2.1).

REFERENCES

Abe, J. (2020). Beyond cultural competence, toward social transformation: Liberation psychologies and the practice of cultural humility. *Journal of Social Work Education*, 56(4), 696–707.

Bell, C. C., Williamson, J. L., & Chien, P. (2008). Cultural, racial, and ethnic competence and psychiatric diagnosis. *Ethnicity & Inequalities in Health & Social Care, 1*(1), 34–41.

Blackburn, F. (2020). Cultural competence: Toward a more robust conceptualisation. *Public Library Quarterly, 39*(3), 229–245.

Boyle, D. P. & Springer, A. (2008). Toward a cultural competence measure for social work with specific populations. *Journal of Ethnic & Cultural Diversity in Social Work, 9*(3–4), 53–71.

Brouse, C. H. (2007). Promoting discussions about cultural competence in an undergraduate health course. *Health Education Journal, 66*(2), 179–187.

Byrd, C. M. (2023). Cycles of development in learning about identities, diversity, and equity. *Cultural Diversity & Ethnic Minority Psychology, 29*(1), 43–52.

Campinha-Bacote, J., (2018, December 4). Cultural competemility: A paradigm shift in the cultural competence versus cultural humility debate—part I. *OJIN: The Online Journal of Issues in Nursing, 24*(1).

Centers for Disease Control and Prevention. (n.d.). *Cultural competence in health and human services*. https://npin.cdc.gov/pages/cultural-competence#what

Cooke, N. A. (2017). *Information services to diverse populations: Developing culturally competent library professionals*. Libraries Unlimited.

Cooke, N. A., & Hill, R. F. (2017). Considering cultural competence: An annotated resource list. *Knowledge Quest, 45*(3), 54–61.

Cooke, N. A., & Jacobs, J. A. (2018). Diversity and cultural competence in the LIS classroom: A curriculum audit. *Urban Library Journal, 24*(1), 2.

Cross, T. L., Bazron, B. J., Dennis, K. W., Isaacs, M. R. (1998). *Towards a culturally competent system of care: A monograph on effective services for minority children who are severely emotionally disturbed*. CASSP Technical Assistance Center, Georgetown University Child Development Center, Washington, D.C., 1989–1991.

Dean, R. G. (2001). The myth of cross-cultural competence. *Families in Society: Journal of Contemporary Social Services, 82*(6), 623–630.

D'Elia, T., Black, M., Carpio, B., & Dwyer, J. J. (2009). Cultural competence in public health: The role of peer-professional partnerships. *Ethnicity & Inequalities in Health & Social Care, 2*(3), 4–8.

Elturk, G. (2003). Diversity and cultural competency. *Colorado Libraries, 29*(4), 5–7.

Engseth, E. (2018). Cultural competency: A framework for equity, diversity, and inclusion in the archival profession in the United States. *The American Archivist, 81*(2), 460–482.

Farrelly, D., Kaplin, D., & Hernandez, D. (2022). A transformational approach to developing cultural humility in the classroom. *Teaching of Psychology, 49*(2), 185–190.

Foronda, C., Baptiste, D.-L., Reinholdt, M. M., & Ousman, K. (2016). Cultural humility: A concept analysis. *Journal of Transcultural Nursing, 27*(3), 210–217.

Getgen, C. (2022). Cultural humility in the LIS profession. *Journal of Academic Librarianship, 48*(4), article 102538.

Gillson, S., & Cherian, N. (2019). The importance of teaching cultural diversity in baccalaureate nursing education. *Journal of Cultural Diversity, 26*(3), 85–88.

Hodge, T. (2019). Integrating cultural humility into public services librarianship. *International Information & Library Review, 51*(3), 268–274.

Hurley, D. A., Kostelecky, S. R., & Townsend, L. (2019). Cultural humility in libraries. *Reference Services Review, 47*(4), 544–555.

Kumagai, A. K., & Lypson, M. L. (2009). Beyond cultural competence: Critical consciousness, social justice, and multicultural education. *Academic Medicine: Journal of the Association of American Medical Colleges, 84*(6), 782–787.

Kumasi, K. D., & Hill, R. F. (2019). What does cultural competence mean to preservice school librarians? A critical discourse analysis. *Social Justice and Cultural Competency: Essential Readings for School Librarians, 64*.

Lawrence, C., Zuckerman, M., Smith, B., & Liu, J. (2012). Building cultural competence in the child welfare workforce: A mixed-methods analysis. *Journal of Public Child Welfare, 6*(2), 225–241.

Lekas, H. M., Pahl, K, Lewis, C. F. (2020, December). Rethinking cultural competence: Shifting to cultural humility. *Health Services Insights, 13*(1), 1–4.

Markey, K., Prosen, M., Martin, E., & Repo Jamal, H. (2021). Fostering an ethos of cultural humility development in nurturing inclusiveness and effective intercultural team working. *Journal of Nursing Management, 29*(8), 2724–2728.

Matteliano, M. A., & Stone, J. H. (2014). Cultural competence education in university rehabilitation programs. *Journal of Cultural Diversity, 21*(3), 112–118.

Moon, S. H., Morgan, T., & Sandage, S. J. (2018). The need for intercultural competence assessment and training among police officers. *Journal of Forensic Psychology Research & Practice, 18*(5), 337–351.

Morris, V. J. (2006, December). *A seat at the table: Seeking culturally competent pedagogy in librarian education*. Association of Library and Information Educators Conference, Seattle, WA.

Naidoo, J. C. (2014). *Diversity programming for digital youth: Promoting cultural competence in the children's library*. ABC-CLIO.

National Association of Social Workers (2015). *Standards and indicators for cultural competence in social work practice*. https://www.socialworkers.org/LinkClick.aspx?fileticket=PonPTDEBrn4%3d&portalid=0

Overall, P. M. (2009). Cultural competence: A conceptual framework for library and information science professionals. *The Library Quarterly, 79*(2), 175–204.

Overall, P. M., Nuñez, A. V., & Reyes-Escudero, V. (2015). *Latinos in libraries, museums, and archives: Cultural competence in action! An asset-based approach*. Rowman & Littlefield.

Press, N. O., & Diggs-Hobson, M. (2005). Providing health information to community members where they are: Characteristics of the culturally competent librarian. *Library Trends, 53*(3), 397–410.

Tahir, F. (2020). How to (un)-learn cultural (in)-competency in social work: A critical discourse analysis of cultural competency trainings in community mental health. *Social Work & Policy Studies, 3*(1), 1–33.

Tervalon, M., & Murray-Garcia, J. (1998). Cultural humility versus cultural competence: A critical distinction in defining physician training outcomes in multicultural education. *Journal of Health Care for the Poor and Underserved, 9*(2), 117–125.

Villagran, M. A. L., & Hawamdeh, S. (2020). Cultural competence in LIS education: Case study of United States ranked schools. *Multicultural Education Review, 12*(2), 136–155.

Yancu, C. & Farmer, D. (2017). Product or process: Cultural competence or cultural humility? *Palliative Medicine and Hospice Care Open Journal, 3*(1), e1–e4.

Young, M. Y., Chan, K. J., Vandette, M.-P., Cherner, R., Hatchard, T., Shah, D., & Kogan, C. S. (2022). Evaluating the organizational cultural competence of a clinical psychology training clinic: Findings and implications for training sites. *Canadian Journal of Community Mental Health, 41*(2), 81–90.

3

The Role of Cultural Humility in Health Care

Kammi Y. Sayaseng

One of the best compliments health care providers (HCPs) can get from their patients is compliance. Without compliance, outcomes cannot be optimized or aligned with the best treatment plan. Building patient compliance starts with a good rapport and relationships. One might ask how an HCP builds a good rapport with his or her patients. Respectful provider/patient interaction with focused listening is one possibility. HCPs who listen with eye contact and engaged body language make patients feel heard and understood. Maaks et al. (2019) discussed how to establish relationship-based communication with pediatric patients and their families utilizing three phases: (1) establishment, (2) development, and (3) engagement. In the first phase, the HCP *establishes* a safe and supportive atmosphere. The HCP then *develops* reflective listening while eliciting the patient's narrative and perspective. In the final phase, the HCP *engages* the patient by sharing the diagnosis, collaboratively developing the plan of care, and ending the visit with a closure.

People often greet others by asking "How are you?" without pausing to hear the response before quickly walking away. HCPs who do not pause and listen cannot fully capture what the patients are communicating or make them feel validated. Unfortunately, time constraints force HCPs to effectively listen as best as they can, often during brief appointments that sometimes include the presence of language interpreters. According to the 2020 U.S. Census, the U.S. population is more racially and ethnically diverse as compared to 2010. Thirteen percent of U.S. residents are foreign born (Maaks et al., 2019).

California ranked second out of fifty-one states with the highest diversity index (69.7 percent) compared to Hawaii's first-place finish (76.0 percent). Of the residents in Fresno County aged five years or older, nearly 19 percent did not speak English well. Spanish, Hmong, and Punjabi were the top non-English languages spoken at the residents' homes (Census Bureau's American Community Survey, 2017).

WHY PRACTICING CULTURAL HUMILITY IS IMPORTANT

Given the diverse population of the United States, HCPs must nurture cross-cultural communication to reduce health disparities, improve access to better care, and promote health equity. Achieving these goals requires understanding and practicing cultural humility. HCPs must be open and willing to rise above personal satisfaction or status. Rick Warren summed it up best: "Humility is not thinking less of yourself; it is thinking of yourself less" (2022).

Severson et al. (1999) described activities of a Transcultural Patient Care Committee (TPCC), with its aim to develop the knowledge and skills of medical center staff to provide culturally congruent care. Some of the activities addressed by the authors included staff development offerings, a transcultural patient care resource manual, and communication and assessment tools. These activities provided a foundation to assist staff with meeting the challenge of caring for multicultural patients. The TPCC was created in 1991 by several nurses with the purpose of enhancing patient care by (a) exploring beliefs and cultural heritage and their influence on values, beliefs, and practices; (b) increasing knowledge and understanding about culturally specific needs of patients; (c) developing multicultural assessment skills in clinical practice; and (d) applying research to clinical practice. The TPCC included representation from African American, Arab, Asian, European, Hispanic, and Midwestern cultures. The committee consisted of members from multidisciplinary teams, including physicians, nurses, social workers, language department staff, chaplains, dieticians, and physical therapists.

Nowadays, we do not typically see such hospital committees as described in this study. Instead, staff training in cultural competence is handled in medical and nursing schools, health-related professional associations, government entities, or via other avenues. The rationale for this training is that providers' knowledge of other cultures, apart from their own, can improve communication skills and enable them to establish rapport with their patients. However, Lekas, Pahl, and Lewis (2020) cautioned that this training, no matter how commendable, can foster implicit racist attitudes and behaviors. For this reason, the authors proposed that providers be trained in cultural humility rather than cultural competence.

CULTURAL BELIEFS AND HEALING PRACTICES

A key element to cultural humility in the health-care setting is provider sensitivity, which recognizes the cultural differences among patients. Understanding that every patient encounter is a cultural meeting, HCPs must be willing to align their attitudes and behaviors with patients' perspectives rather than their own. Where values and practices vary greatly, it is more difficult to gain trust, thus increasing the likelihood of noncompliance and subsequent negative health outcomes.

Acknowledging different cultural practices and the use of complementary and alternative medicines (CAM) can benefit HCPs in their pursuit of cultural sensitivity in the clinical setting. In Eastern Asia, some examples of CAM use include acupuncture, herbal remedies, moxibustion, coining, and cupping. Moreover, the Chinese cultural belief of yin and yang, or the opposing forces, explains the importance of balancing the two forces within one's system to achieve harmony or health (Dashtdar et al., 2016). After giving birth, many Chinese women will ask for warm water to drink. Salads will be left untouched since they are considered a cold food that will further imbalance the system. In traditional Chinese medicine, the wind is considered the root cause of many diseases (Dashtdar et al., 2016). Within Arab families, men prefer male providers and women prefer female providers. Men will accompany women to appointments and will often "speak" for the female patient. Hispanics utilize massage, herbal remedies, and folk healers (Maaks et al., 2019). In the past, practices such as coining, cupping, and moxibustion were widely misunderstood within American culture, leading to instances where HCPs would occasionally file child abuse claims against families.

POWER IMBALANCES: LEARNING AND REFLECTING

Patient Differences and Power Imbalances

HCPs are highly regarded in most cultures. Among the chief reasons people enter the health-care field is to help others, ease suffering, and improve lives. As Rick Warren (2022) wrote, "Kindness always starts with noticing the needs and hurts of others." However, the desire to help others must include cultural humility to be most effective. Cultural humility involves learning about patients' differences and addressing the power imbalance between provider and patient, secondary to language barriers and/or cultural differences.

I have been a pediatric nurse practitioner (PNP) since 2000, working with patients from a wide variety of cultures and backgrounds. I recall one memorable patient I saw during the wintertime. This infant had severe atopic dermatitis, commonly known as eczema, and was of Mixteco descent. Mixteco is an Indigenous Mesoamerican population from the Mexican states of Oaxaca,

Guerrero, and Michoacan. The parents were also Mixteco but spoke only Spanish. I communicated with them in Spanish while coordinating the infant's dermatological care and treatments. The infant's skin was dry and peeling from head to toe and bleeding in some areas. One of the treatments recommended for severe atopic dermatitis is wet wrap therapy. The dermatologist and I recommended that the parents dampen a 100 percent cotton pajama and put that on the infant (after applying the prescribed topical steroid and emollient), followed by another layer of dry cotton pajamas. The infant was to wear this overnight, and it would be taken off upon waking the next morning. The idea was to remove the dead skin from his body, rehydrate the healthy skin, and increase the systemic absorption of the topical steroids and emollients. In teaching the parents this treatment, we instructed them to perform it every day, beginning at bedtime. The parents agreed to our plan and went home with instructions.

In the follow-up visit two weeks later, we noticed that the infant's skin condition had not improved. When we inquired about how many times and for how many hours the parents were utilizing the treatment plan, they admitted they had not followed our instructions because they feared it would give their infant pneumonia. They acknowledged initially agreeing to the treatment plan out of respect but explained that in their culture, wearing wet clothes to bed, especially in the winter, would almost certainly result in pneumonia. Upon hearing their concerns, we made some accommodations. We asked if the parents would be willing to try the wet pajama wrap therapy in the spring, during the daytime, and for about three to four hours at a time, a few days per week. The parents were willing to do this, provided their child did not have to go to sleep in wet clothes. At the next follow-up visit, the child's skin condition improved.

This case demonstrates the necessity to learn how cultural differences can create power imbalances within patient/provider relationships. Cultural variations also reveal differing or unknown perceptions of health and illness. Southeast Asians and Hispanics (especially Indigenous populations) will not challenge HCPs. To avoid the appearance of being disrespectful, they prefer to say "yes" to everything rather than "no" (Sayaseng, 2018). Some patients follow instructions exactly as told. Others prefer to avoid eye contact, because to do otherwise is considered disrespectful.

Power Imbalances between Health-Care Providers and Patients

Sayaseng (2018) discussed a case involving a five-day-old Southeast Asian (Laotian) male that demonstrated cultural differences and power imbalances between the health-care provider and the patient. The newborn presented with his parents to an outpatient clinic for a follow-up hospital discharge. As the author of this study, I personally encountered this case as I was the provider who attended to the newborn and his parents that day. The parents, who were in their early thirties, had recently migrated and spoke limited English, and this was their first child. They did not have any local family or friends for support. Before hospital discharge, the parents indicated to hospital staff that they wished to do exclusive breastfeeding. The father informed me in Lao that hospital staff had told them to breastfeed every three to four hours.

On the day of the exam, the newborn's weight was 8.5 percent below birth weight on day five of life. Newborns are expected to regain their birth weight by ten to fourteen days of life. Upon further inquiry, the parents stated that they had to give the newborn formula because he would not latch on to the mother's breast to feed due to excessive crying. When asked why they thought their baby was crying so much, the parents did not know. They told me they were following the discharge instructions from the hospital, to feed their baby "every three to four hours." However, breastfeeding does not follow a schedule like formula-feeding does. Instead, it should happen on demand, and when the baby wants to feed, the mother should put the baby to the breast. I asked the father if they understood the hospital's discharge instructions, to which he replied, "Somewhat, but we did not want to question the staff."

This case demonstrates how some cultures will follow medical instructions extremely carefully, even in the presence of unwelcome conditions. The parents waited precisely "every three to four hours" to feed their baby, even when the hospital staff was incorrect in advising the mother to breastfeed her newborn every three to four hours. These first-time parents did not understand feeding schedules, as breastfeeding should occur whenever the infant exhibits signs of hunger. Though I listened and understood their story and discussed with them why their newborn was crying so much, the parents had already decided to continue with only formula feeding. This was unfortunate, as breastfeeding carries strong benefits for both baby and mother.

CULTURAL BELIEFS AND HEALTH CARE: OPENNESS VERSUS EGOISM AMONG HEALTH-CARE PROVIDERS

As an associate professor of pediatric nursing and a PNP primary care provider, I often encounter students who raise questions about the boundaries of child abuse or neglect when families have different beliefs regarding health care. This question is valid and crucial for HCPs, as there is no single correct answer. Each case and patient is unique and deserves individualized care and consideration.

I first became aware of potential clashes between Western medicine and cultural humility in health care while training to become a registered nurse (RN). A seven-year-old Hmong boy presented with clubfeet, and the parents were refusing corrective surgery because they felt that the "spirits" had given their son clubfeet for a wrong done by an ancestor. Fixing their son's clubfeet could cause the family major health and financial disasters, according to the family's lawyer. In the first court ruling, Western medicine prevailed, and the judge approved the corrective surgery. However, the same judge reversed his own ruling ten months later after consulting with a psychiatrist and was quoted as saying, "A Southeast Asian boy shouldn't be forced to have surgery because his family's fear of arousing angry spirits would do him more harm than skipping operations to fix his club feet." After the second ruling, the mother, through an interpreter, summarized cultural humility in health care fittingly by stating in the local newspaper, "I think the judge or everybody has to know more about people before making a judgement. They have to respect … respect the people. We are different" (Bigham, 1990). Hmong people come from the mountainous northern part of Laos. Before the Vietnam War in the early 1970s, when Hmong people were helping the Americans fight communist insurgents, many of these people had experienced little of the outside world. After the war, many Hmong fled to Thailand for refuge before ultimately arriving in the United States.

Patients from certain cultural and religious groups may decline blood transfusions due to fear of blood-borne diseases, problems or reactions with previous transfusions, and a preference to get blood only when absolutely necessary. Another reason for transfusion refusal is alloimmunization, or an immune response to foreign antigens from another human (Crookston, 2022). Jehovah's Witnesses are known to decline blood transfusions, and as of 2020, there were over one million active Jehovah's Witnesses in North America. Rather than "generalize" this population, HCPs need to discuss this situation with these patients beforehand when possible as each person and case is unique. Providers need to explain in detail the consequences of not undergoing a blood transfusion when it is medically indicated.

Be Free from Judgment and Assumptions

Buddhist teaching says, "Do not be the judge of people; do not make assumptions about others. A person is destroyed by holding judgments about others" (Buddhist teaching, n.d.). Having been raised in a two-culture family, I empathize with the patient situations previously mentioned. Rick Warren's (2022) quote on humility resonates well with the teachings I received from my parents: "Be humble about yourself. When you think you know and have it all, there's bound to be someone who knows and has more than you do." My family migrated to the United States in 1984, and except for my parents, all of my family members spoke English before our arrival. When we first settled here, people often asked me if I spoke English. Until I was asked recently, I had not thought about my ability to speak English in a very long time, so it caught me by surprise. The question came from an elderly RN visiting my home, and I simply answered with a short "Yes." I did not think about it much at the time, nor did I find it offensive until I relayed the incident to my friends, who all agreed it was a rude question to ask.

Part of being culturally humble involves self-reflection or self-evaluation. As I reflected on the incident, I recognized that deep down, I felt offended that someone would assume I did not speak English just because I looked different from them. This incident reminded me of a comment an acquaintance made to me when I was in my teens: "I have not seen an Asian with curly hair before. Is your hair naturally curly?" I had, and still have, naturally curly long hair. As I was processing the question, I was thinking, "Where have you been that you have not seen an Asian with curly hair before?" These two personal incidents taught me that people make assumptions about others based on their own experiences. As HCPs, we must refrain from making assumptions about patients who are different from us. We should not assume that "our way" is "the only way" to care for patients and their families. It is critical that we be able to look past a person's skin color and treat all patients equally and with respect, thereby recognizing our own subconscious biases. Cultural humility is a lifelong commitment to learning and encouraging self-evaluation and self-criticism (Campinha-Bacote, 2018).

Caring for Youth with Special Health-Care Needs (CYSHCN)

Kuo and Turchi (2022) defined children and youth with special health-care needs (CYSHCN) as children and youth under twenty-one years of age who have or are at an increased risk of developing a chronic physical, developmental, behavioral, or emotional condition that requires health and related services beyond what is usually involved. Their special health-care needs represent a broad range of complex health conditions. There are three main concepts of care that must be embraced for CYSHCN: (1) patients and their families are active and core participants in their plans of care and decision-making; (2) all services are provided in a culturally competent, linguistically appropriate, and accessible manner; and (3) all care is evidence based (Kuo & Turchi 2022).

I have worked with colleagues who have children with special health-care needs, and they have frequently encountered bias among HCPs who do not acknowledge or address patients' uniqueness or cultural needs. This is not intended to suggest that insensitivity always leads to demeaning treatment but rather to emphasize the importance of open-mindedness and caution when making assumptions. Actively listening to patients and their parents and involving them in their plans of care promotes understanding, sensitivity, and better outcomes. Children and youth with special health-care needs depend on medical and community-based services to survive and thrive.

A Patient's Ultimate Compliment: Compliance

According to the Centers for Disease Control and Prevention (CDC, 2022), deaths related to pregnancy complications are rare in the United States. However, about seven hundred women die from such tragic outcomes each year (CDC, 2022). Within this unfortunate statistic is the presence of significant racial disparities. Specifically, American Indian, Alaska Native, and Black women are two to three times more likely to die of pregnancy-related causes compared to their Caucasian counterparts. This raises an important question: Why do such disparities still persist despite the advances in medical care? One contributing factor is that some HCPs do not take the complaints of these women seriously—they do not listen intently or hear their concerns. HCPs who offer respectful and culturally sensitive care receive respect in return. That respect might represent compliance, which promotes successful interventions and better health outcomes.

Clinical Pearls for Providing Cultural Humility in Care

In conclusion, the following quote eloquently sums up cultural humility within the health-care field: "Do not be the judge of people; do not make assumptions about others. A person is destroyed by holding judgments about others" (Buddhist teaching, n.d.). Health-care providers who exhibit judgment or preconceived notions about their patients most certainly will not have successful patient/provider relationships. This is not a benign, innocuous matter. Poor relationships jeopardize treatment compliance and can lead to negative or unwanted health outcomes. Cultural humility in health care must come from a collective effort of all involved—CPs and patients. To ensure fewer conflicts between Western medicine and patients' beliefs and to promote positive health outcomes, both providers and patients need to cultivate open attitudes and open ears.

REFERENCES

Bigham, J. (1990). *Judge rules against corrective surgery for boy whose religion forbids it*. Associated Press News. https://apnews.com/article/c0f093b7d7254446422fce4c93514e74

Buddhist teaching. (n.d.). Do not be the judge of people; do not make assumptions about others. A person is destroyed by holding judgments about others. https://www.azquotes.com/quote/768820

Campinha-Bacote, J. (2018). Cultural competemility: A paradigm shift in the cultural competence versus cultural humility debate—part I. *The Online Journal of Issues in Nursing, 24*(1). 10.3912/OJIN.Vol24No01PPT20

Census Bureau's American Community Survey. (2017). *ACS demographic and housing estimates*. https://data.census.gov/cedsci/table?tid=ACSDP5Y2017.DP05&g=0400000US06_0500000US06019

Centers for Disease Control and Prevention. (2022). *Pregnancy related deaths in the United States*. https://www.cdc.gov/hearher/pregnancy-related-deaths/

Crookston, K. P. (2022). *The approach to the patient who declines blood transfusion*. https://www.uptodate.com/contents/the-approach-to-the-patient-who-declines-blood-transfusion?search=The%20approach%20to%20the

%20patient%20who%20declines%20blood%20transfusion&source=search_result&selectedTitle=1~150&usage_type=default&display_rank=1

Dashtdar, M., Dashtdar, M. R., Dashtdar, B., Kardi, K., & Shirazi, M. K. (2016). The concept of wind in traditional Chinese medicine. *Journal of Pharmacopuncture, 19*(4), 293–302. https://doi.org/10.3831/KPI.2016.19.030

Kuo, D. Z., & Turchi, R. M. (2022). *Children and youth with special health care needs.* https://www.uptodate.com/contents/children-and-youth-with-special-health-care-needs?search=health%20care%20for%20special%20needs%20children%20&source=search_result&selectedTitle=1~31&usage_type=default&display_rank=1

Lekas, H. M., Pahl, K., & Lewis, C. F. (2020). Rethinking cultural competence: Shifting to cultural humility. *Health Services Insights*, 13. DOI: 10.1177/1178632920970580

Maaks, D. L. G., Starr, N. B., Brady, M. A., Gaylord, N. M., Driessnack, M., & Duderstadt, K. (2019). *Burns' pediatric primary care* (7th ed.). Elsevier.

Sayaseng, K. Y. (2018). Breastfeeding support and counseling: A practical guide for the general practitioners in outpatient clinics. *International Journal of Studies in Nursing, 3*(3). https://doi.org/10.20849/ijsn.v3i3.459

Severson, M., Leinonen, S., Matt-Hensrud, N., & Ruegg, J. (1999). Transcultural patient care committee: Actualization concepts and developing skills. *Journal for Nurses in Staff Development (JNSD)*. 15(4), 141–147. ISSN: 1098-7886

Warren, R. (2022). *The purpose driven life quotes.* https://www.goodreads.com/work/quotes/2265235-the-purpose-driven-life-what-on-earth-am-i-here-for

4

Health Literacy

BRIDGING THE GAP

Teresa Wagner and Rachel Walden

Public libraries traditionally serve as a resource for swift and timely delivery of up-to-date and accurate information for a variety of topics (Heimlich, 2014). Consumer health information has traditionally been the responsibility of medical libraries. However, since medical libraries tend to have limited access and scope, public libraries have more recently engaged in initiatives to enhance community health information and services (Malachowski, 2014).

Librarians can add value to typical core services through additional functions applicable to their patrons' needs, such as building individual, family, and community health capacity that bridges information gaps by providing health-literate, community-based information (Heimlich, 2014). Increasing community capacity by providing usable health information stands to improve health and wellness decisions while at the same time empowering individuals with limited resources to understand health care better. By enhancing health literacy, these services also enhance cultural humility and health equity (Lie et al., 2012).

Many different things make up who we are, including differences in values, beliefs, and life experiences. There are many diverse parts of our identities and several distinctive types of cultural differences. When thinking about culture, we often limit our thoughts to national origin and ethnicity, but culture goes much deeper and continues to expand in definition (Lie et al., 2012). Though language is one type of cultural difference, there are many other types, including gender, national origin, religion or faith, family, education, and so on. The different types of cultures give us identities that are dynamic and unique. Our cultural differences influence our viewpoints, the way we see the world, and how we communicate with others (Lie et al., 2012).

Culture is:

- learned and transmitted by members of our community,
- dynamic and changes with time,
- integrated from diverse aspects of our lives,
- our framework for action (EuroMed Info, 2021).

Knowing someone's culture does not mean we can predict their beliefs, values, or behavior. Upon self-reflection, which aspects of your culture and identity shape how you see yourself? How do others see you? How do you communicate and prefer to communicate with others? Cultural framework impacts not only our everyday lives but also how we experience health care (EuroMed Info, 2021).

When considering culture in the health-care setting, each cultural group brings its own perspectives and values. Many health beliefs and health practices differ from those of the traditional American health-care culture (EuroMed Info, 2021). These can include:

- attitudes about medical care,
- meaning of a diagnosis,
- ability to understand and manage illness,
- ability to cope with the course of illness,
- consequences of medical treatment.

The expectation of many health-care professionals has been that patients will conform to mainstream values (Lie et al., 2012). Imagine what it would be like if your answers to the previous questions about your culture and identity inhibited your access to the information and services you needed to make important health decisions for you and your family. Unfortunately, too many people have had this experience and usually have suffered health disparities as a result.

Health literacy has historically been defined as "the capacity to understand basic health information and make appropriate health decisions." According to the Institute of Medicine (IOM), individuals with low levels of health literacy face challenges in making informed choices about the best health and health-care options for themselves and their families (IOM, 2011). The Agency for Healthcare Research and Quality added, "9 out of 10 Americans may lack the knowledge and skills needed to manage their health and prevent disease (AHRQ, 2011)." Those populations most at risk for low health literacy include the elderly and people with low socioeconomic status and education attainment, as well as limited English proficiency (IOM, 2011). This definition focuses on the abilities of individuals and individual approaches to health literacy.

Healthy People 2030 expanded the definition of health literacy to include organizational health literacy along with the traditional personal health literacy as previous definitions posited (ODPHP, n.d.). From the organizational health literacy perspective, health care delivered without attention to linguistic and cultural diversity causes barriers and inequities where those unable to understand health-care instructions or access health care due to linguistic and cultural differences may experience diminished health outcomes (ODPHP, n.d.). This new definition represents a shift from focusing on low health literacy as a characteristic of individual patients to an understanding that organizations, such as hospitals, and other health-care providers have a responsibility to ensure understanding regardless of the patient's individual background or literacy level.

The IOM reports call for practice interventions to increase "cultural and linguistic competency" to reduce disparate treatment of underrepresented groups from medical professionals who are unaware of how their cultural bias affects their patients (IOM, 2011). While intentional racism and other biases can certainly exist among health-care providers, in some cases where this lack of awareness may result from cultural miscommunication, implicit bias, and the health literacy gap, positive change may be more readily achievable (McCann et al., 2013). Implicit bias, the positive or negative mental attitude that a person holds at an unconscious level toward a person or group, although subtle and often unintentional, manifests into disparate treatment (McCann et al., 2013). Research has shown that providers with higher levels of implicit bias have lower levels of administering appropriate treatment (Sawaya, 2019). However, cultural sensitivity involves more than just providing an interpreter for patients who require one. Providing patients with translators, along with cultural humility that meets people where they live, can minimize disparate health outcomes and achieve good health-care interventions for all people. Effective training strategies empower health professionals to recognize and address these problems (McCann et al., 2013). Adopting cultural humility is the best approach toward understanding culture. It is interactive and requires good listening skills, including:

- approaching people with openness to learn,
- asking open-ended questions rather than making assumptions,
- striving to understand rather than to inform,
- requiring a commitment to lifelong learning, continuous self-reflection on one's own assumptions and practices,
- being comfortable with "not knowing," and recognizing the power/privilege imbalance that exists between patients and health professionals (Tervalon & Murray-Garcia, 1998, 117-123).

Cultural humility commands the "ability to maintain an interpersonal stance that is other-oriented (or open to the other) in relation to aspects of cultural identity that are most important to the [person]" (Hook et al., 2013, 2). Recommendations include: (1) ask patients open-ended questions and follow their lead about "appropriate ways to facilitate communication within families and between families and other health care providers"; (2) plan, write, and design materials to reflect the audience, and be as inclusive as possible; and (3) use plain language universally to address cultural, linguistic, and functional challenges (EuroMed Info, 2021). All libraries can help health-care providers address cultural humility issues by providing access to implicit bias programming to medical professional schools and training programs lending a third-party and confidential perspective to facilitate a willingness to be vulnerable, to conduct an audit of self and form openness to address biases as well as develop dedication to this lifelong process (Singh, 2020). Libraries can also serve as cultural knowledge hubs by selecting books and other resources that address bias and culture in health care, removing collection materials that may promote harmful stereotypes or misinformation, and promoting these materials to health-care providers, administrators, and trainees.

When addressing personal health literacy, developing health literacy skills can help individuals overcome the bias in treatment they receive (Lie et al., 2012). The American Medical Association found that poor health literacy is a "stronger predictor of a person's health than age, income, employment status, education level and race" (AMA, 1999). At the American Library Association 2019 Midwinter Meeting, titled "Implicit Bias, Health Disparities and Health Literacy: Intersections in Health Equity," Michele Spatz from the Network of the National Library of Medicine (NNLM) stated that "our healthcare system continues to become more complex and fragmented. Individuals must assume greater responsibility for self-care. At the same time, our society actively markets unhealthy lifestyles, and our educational systems do not really teach health literacy skills, such as how to access, understand, assess, and use information to improve personal health" (Sawaya, 2019). Addressing individual aspects of health literacy can include information literacy programs, which can be offered by public libraries as part of their core services, or by academic or medical libraries through outreach and other programs and services targeted directly to patients.

The NNLM has taken the lead in transforming libraries as the conduit to health literacy, helping to bridge the gap consumers experience in health-literate information, especially in underserved areas. Their annual outreach grants go a long way in engaging communities and impacting populations that suffer from severe health disparities or experience higher rates of low health literacy (NNLM, 2021). For example, NNLM grant funding led to foundational research to inform and improve organizational health literacy through an evaluation of hospitals across north Texas (Howe et al., 2020), which resulted in the development of Innovate to Communicate, a workshop and tool kit for health-care entities to improve their health-literate practices (CDC, 2021). Other grants have been instrumental in addressing personal health literacy, such as the Memphis Health Outreach and Connect Crew that partners with local schools, community centers, parks, and service providers to bring a robust variety of programming for all ages and learning levels to communities without access to traditional library programs on health literacy and wellness (NNLM Memphis, 2021).

The NNLM key initiatives aim to (1) develop approaches to promote awareness of, improve access to, and enable use of NNLM's resources and data; (2) develop and support a diverse workforce to access information resources and data and support data-driven research; and (3) provide community-driven innovative approaches and interventions for biomedical and health information access and use (NNLM Initiatives, 2021). The network also offers training for MedlinePlus.gov (produced by the National Library of Medicine) to aid public and other libraries in directing individuals to reliable online sources of health information, as well as training on topics related to both health literacy and cultural humility.

Another way in which libraries can aid in countering limited health literacy is by providing reliable access to the internet and training on evaluating health information online. The Pew Internet and American Life Project revealed that even though people turn to health professionals for health-related information, an estimated 80 percent of internet users prefer it online (Beschnett & Bulger, 2013). Even though the Healthy People 2020 goals hoped to expand nationwide internet access on health-connected websites by 10 percent (Malachowski, 2011), many rural and underserved areas still lack any access to online health information. As a result, many people access low-cost online services and ask health-related questions at their local library (Borman, 2013).

Public libraries are unique community organizations positioned to both offset this internet access gap and provide training and resources relevant to their specific communities served. Understanding community needs and participating more fully in addressing them affords libraries a significant opportunity to not only contribute to public health initiatives but also build cultural humility on both sides of the health-care equation (Naccarella & Horwood, 2021). Michele Spatz encouraged public libraries to better understand community needs; engage with other community-based organizations, health-care educators, and providers who embrace health-literacy programming; and work to develop new programming in their libraries (Sawaya, 2019). In line with Healthy People 2030, libraries are positioned to help combat health literacy as a public health issue by increasing health literacy in their communities, which has proven to be an effective tool in addressing health disparities for vulnerable communities (Naccarella & Horwood, 2021).

For example, one library in Jeff Davis County, Texas, has addressed childhood hunger and health literacy in its rural communities by providing meals and health information for children and their families, in addition to training library staff in these issues. The program has thereby improved the nutritional literacy of children through library-based activities, summer reading programs, and increased physical activity. The area served is not only a literal desert but also a food desert since the schools do not have cafeterias, nor are they part of the National School Lunch or Breakfast Programs. Between the Food Pantry of Jeff Davis County and the library's Kids Pantry, lunch is provided to 70 percent of all children under eighteen in the county. A "Mobile Comunidad" bus also goes out to the community to provide these same services to those without transportation (Perrault, 2021). Another public library in Pottsboro, Texas, partnered with health-care services in an urban area through Telehealth, dedicating a room in the library for their community members to receive confidential health-care appointments. The library also provides Wi-Fi and resources for community members without online access to health and other types of information (Pottsboro Area Library, 2022).

Programs that build workforce capacity in the form of community health workers (CHWs) have also begun partnering with libraries. Since libraries serve as the social and informational center of the community in many rural and underserved areas, these partnerships can help libraries identify natural helpers in the community and refer them to state and federally funded programs held by academia or community-based organizations. In return, the identified participants receive training and certification (depending on the state) as community health workers and can be employed in the library or in another entity within the area to help provide much-needed health-literacy services (Texas Higher Education Coordinating Board, 2021).

Research also suggests that managing and providing health information, as well as assisting patients in navigating health-care services (commonly known as patient navigation), can exhibit overlapping responsibilities among CHWs, health sciences librarians, and patient navigators (RHIhub, 2020). Building workforce capacity in the form of patient navigators may also provide an avenue for collaboration with libraries to meet community needs for health literacy (Nix et al., 2016).

In academic and medical libraries, contributions to improve health literacy and cultural humility can take many forms, including collection development, programming, acting as a conduit for instruction of health-care providers and trainees, consumer health outreach, and research. Health sciences librarians have led research on health literacy that could be used to inform and improve organizational health literacy, such as an evaluation of patient-oriented COVID-19 information produced by state health departments (Mani et al., 2021). Medical librarians are often involved in outreach addressing personal health literacy, such as those in Appalachia where patient-friendly health information handouts were delivered to free clinic events with careful attention to the community's needs and interests (Weyant et al., 2019). In 2021, the Medical University of South Carolina's libraries, along with Hands on Health South Carolina, hosted the inaugural Southeast Health Literacy conference, offering training and dialogue on health literacy and equity to a variety of health-related professionals throughout the region (Southeast Health Literacy Conference, 2021). Many academic and medical libraries offer workshops and internet access for the public as well, particularly at state institutions that provide access to the public.

Overall, libraries can address health inequities through partnerships with academic institutions, community-based organizations, and health entities in their communities. By learning more about the needs of their communities and training staff about the resources available to meet those needs, libraries can adopt inclusive health programming and services to engage with vulnerable populations and proactively reach out to those in the community to minimize disparate treatment. "Health literacy is the librarian's health equity tool" (Sawaya, 2019).

At the same time, libraries can help health-care providers address cultural humility issues that are complex and involve critically engaging with biases (Singh, 2020). Providing access to implicit bias programming within these partnerships to address health inequities can lend a third-party and confidential perspective to facilitate providers' willingness to be vulnerable, to conduct an audit of themselves, and to be willing to address their biases as well as be dedicated to this lifelong process. This is not easy, simple, prescriptive, or comfortable (Singh, 2020). To enhance cultural humility and facilitate equitable delivery of health care with minimal bias, the library can help bridge the gap between patrons and health information and between patients and providers.

REFERENCES

Agency for Healthcare Research & Quality (AHRQ). (2011). *Health literacy interventions and outcomes: An updated systematic review.* Evidence Report 199. https://www.ahrq.gov/downloads/pub/evidence/pdf/literacy/literacyup.pdf

American Medical Association (AMA). (1999). Health literacy: Report of the Council on Scientific Affairs. Ad Hoc Committee on Health Literacy for the Council on Scientific Affairs. *Journal of the American Medical Association, 281*(6), 552–557.

Beschnett, A., & Bulger, J. (2013). Patient education and the hospital library: Opportunities for involvement. *Journal of Hospital Librarianship, 13*(1), 42–46. doi:10.1080/15323269.2013.743350

Borman, L. D. (2013). Studying up on health care literacy. *American Libraries, 44*(11), 42–43.

Centers for Disease Control (CDC). (2021). Health Literacy. Innovate to Communicate. https://www.cdc.gov/healthliteracy/non-cdc-training.html#health-literacy

EuroMed Info. (2021). Impact of culture on patient education. https://www.euromedinfo.eu/impact-of-culture-on-patient-education-introduction.html/

Heimlich, S. L. (2014). New and emerging roles for medical librarians. *Journal of Hospital Librarianship, 14*(1), 24–32. doi:10.1080/15323269.2014.859995

Hook, J. N., Davis, D. E., Owen, J., Worthington, E. L., & Utsey, S. O. (2013). Cultural humility: Measuring openness to culturally diverse clients. *Journal of Counseling Psychology, 60*(3), 353–366. https://doi.org/10.1037/a0032595

Howe, C. J., Adame, T., Lewis, B., & Wagner, T. (2020). Assessing organizational focus on health literacy in hospitals in North Texas. *American Journal of Nursing, 120*(12), 24–33. https://journals.lww.com/ajnonline/Fulltext/2020/12000/Original_Research Assessing Organizational_Focus.26.aspx

Institute of Medicine (IOM). (2011). *Health literacy implications for health care reform: A workshop summary.* National Academies Press. https://www.ncbi.nlm.nih.gov/books/NBK242436/

Lie, D., Carter-Pokras, O., Braun, B., & Coleman, C. (2012). What do health literacy and cultural competence have in common? Calling for a collaborative pedagogy. *Journal of Health Communication, 17*(03), 13–22. doi:10.1080/10810730.2012.712625

Malachowski, M. (2014). Obamacare and the proper role of public libraries in health literacy. *Computers in Libraries, 34*(1), 4–9.

Malachowski, M. (2011). Public libraries and health literacy. *Computers in Libraries, 31*(10), 5–9.

Mani, N. S., Ottosen, T., Fratta, M., & Yu, F. (2021). "A health literacy analysis of the consumer-oriented COVID-19 information produced by ten state health departments." *Journal of the Medical Library Association, 109*(3), 422–431. doi:10.5195/jmla.2021.1165

McCann, M., Carter-Pokras, O., Braun, B., & Hussein, C. (2013). Cultural competency and health literacy: A guide for teaching health professionals and students. University of Maryland School of Public Health, 1–19.

Naccarella, L., & Horwood, J. (2021). Public libraries as health literate multi-purpose workspaces for improving health literacy. *Health Promotion Journal of Australia, 32*(S1), 29–32. https://doi.org/10.1002/hpja.437

Network of the National Library of Medicine (NNLM). (2021). *An introduction to health literacy.* https://new.nnlm.gov/guides/intro-health-literacy

Network of the National Library of Medicine (NNLM). (2021). *National Initiatives.* https://nnlm.gov/initiatives

Network of the National Library of Medicine (NNLM). (2021). *In Memphis: Health outreach with the Connect Crew.* https://nnlm.gov/funding/funded/memphis-health-outreach-connect-crew

Nix, A. T., Huber, J. T., Shapiro, R. M., & Pfeifle, A. (2016). Examining care navigation: Librarian participation in a teambased approach? *Journal of the Medical Library Association, 104*(2).

Office of Disease Prevention and Health Promotion (ODPHP). (n.d.). *Health literacy in Healthy People 2030*. U.S. Department of Health and Human Services. https://health.gov/our-work/national-health-initiatives/healthy-people/healthy-people-2030/health-literacy-healthy-people-2030

Perrault, A. (2021, April 28). "Mobile Comunidad" puts resources on wheels in Jeff Davis County. *The Big Bend Sentinel*. https://bigbendsentinel.com/2021/04/28/mobile-comunidad-puts-resources-on-wheels-in-jeff-davis-county/

Pottsboro Area Library. (2022). *Health*. https://pottsborolibrary.com/health/

RHIhub. (2020). *Interdisciplinary care teams, patient navigators, and community health workers*. https://www.ruralhealthinfo.org/toolkits/sdoh/2/health-care-settings/care-teams#:~:text=A%20CHW%20serves%20in%20a,improve%20follow%2Dup%20and%20adherence

Sawaya, J. (2019, March 7). *Health literacy: The librarians' tool to address health disparities*. Public Library Association. http://publiclibrariesonline.org/2019/03/health-literacy-the-librarians-tool-to-address-health-disparities/

Singh, R. (2020). Promoting civic engagement through cultivating culturally competent self-reflexive information professionals. *Journal of the Australian Library and Information Association, 69*(3), 302–315. https://doi.org/10.1080/24750158.2020.1777635

Southeast Health Literacy Conference. (2021). https://www.healthliteracyconference.com/

Tervalon, M., & Murray-Garcia, J. (1998). Cultural humility versus cultural competence: A critical distinction in defining physician training outcomes in multicultural education. *Journal of Health Care for the Poor and Underserved, 9*(2), 117–125. https://doi.org/10.1353/hpu.2010.0233

Texas Higher Education Coordinating Board. (2021). *Accelerating credentials of purpose and value 60x30TX Grant Program*. University of North Texas Health Science Center Award: Training and Upskilling CHWs in Texas. https://www.highered.texas.gov/

Weyant, E. C., Woodward, N. J., Walden, R. R., & Wallace, R. L. (2019). Reflections on a Decade of Promoting Consumer Health Resources at Remote Area Medical Clinics. *Journal of Consumer Health on the Internet, 23*(4), 403–410. DOI: 10.1080/15398285.2019.1687198

Part II

Applications in Libraries

5

Overview of Cultural Humility Literature and Research

Erica Brody and Stacey E. Wahl

The American Library Association (ALA) defines the mission of libraries as "forums for information and ideas" (American Library Association, 2006b). Further, "Free access to the books, ideas, resources, and information in America's libraries is imperative for education, employment, enjoyment, and self-government" (American Library Association, 2006a). Emerging as spaces where communities can gather, libraries have the potential to offer digital platforms for the creation, preservation, storage, and sharing of community information in various forms, such as print, audio, and video (Chowdhury et al., 2006; Wood, 2021).

DEFINITION OF CULTURAL HUMILITY

The concept of cultural humility was introduced into the professional literature by Tervalon and Murray-Garcia in 1998 within the context of training physicians to deliver culturally sensitive care to patients from diverse backgrounds. The key elements of cultural humility are (1) self-reflection, (2) a commitment to rectify power imbalances, and (3) acknowledgment of the assets or strengths of individuals and communities to establish "non-paternalistic relationships" with individuals and communities (Tervalon & Murray-Garcia, 1998). In the past twenty-five years, the term "cultural humility" has been adopted by other disciplines, such as psychology, social work, education, and librarianship (Haynes-Mendez & Engelsmeier, 2020; Kangos & Pieterse, 2021; Lekas et al., 2020; Tucker, 2019).

While this term is relatively new to the library literature, elements of cultural humility, such as reflective practice and cultural awareness, can be found in the literature going back several decades (Birdi et al., 2012; Cooper, 2005). For this chapter, we have investigated the library literature for work related to cultural humility, regardless of the terminology used.

The practice of cultural humility can help ensure that libraries and librarians (1) provide culturally sensitive and equitable services to our users, thus contributing to a more socially just society, and (2) work to make the profession of librarianship more welcoming and inclusive of people from diverse backgrounds, in other words, "dewhitening librarianship" (Espinal et al., 2021). Drawing from the literature, we describe how cultural humility enables libraries to fulfill their goals of serving all populations, especially considering that the populations libraries aim to serve are significantly more diverse than the current workforce within libraries. We have examined cultural humility at three levels: intrapersonal, interpersonal, and collective, a framework drawn from an examination of nursing education (Hughes et al., 2020).

CULTURAL HUMILITY—INTRAPERSONAL LEVEL

At the intrapersonal level, cultural humility is an awareness that one's understanding of culture is limited to one's worldview, based on one's life experiences, and complemented by ongoing self-reflection of how one's identity and life experiences influence one's assumptions about others (Hughes et al., 2020). Writing about public services librarianship, Hodge posits, "To provide the best possible service, we must start with ourselves first ... so we can meet our users where they are with as few preconceptions as possible" (Hodge, 2019, 268). We need to reflect on our intersecting identities (e.g., racial, ethnic, gender, etc.) and how they subject us to privilege or oppression within society. Further, we must be willing to undertake the potentially uncomfortable task of identifying our biases, meaning our preferences for or against something when compared to something else. These biases can be explicit (I do not like meat, so I will not eat it) or implicit (I tend to gravitate toward people who look like me in an unfamiliar situation). While difficult, this part of the process is crucial because it provides the foundation for seeking information that enables us to broaden our perspective. Identifying our gaps in understanding and recognizing circumstances where we may be incorrectly interpreting situations, people, or cultures is the first step in changing our perspective. Individuals can use tools such as the Implicit Association Test (Project Implicit) to identify unconscious biases and preferences (Project Implicit, 2011).

Once we identify some of our biases, Hodge describes several techniques to decrease the influence of these biases on our actions. For example, increased self-awareness of instances when we make assumptions about a person based on a stereotype can help us to course-correct in the middle of an interaction and redirect our focus on the individual in front of us instead of allowing our biases to influence the interaction. We are then better able to consider how individual experiences may influence information-seeking practices and needs (Hodge, 2019). To increase cultural humility, Zettervall and Nienow suggest engaging in reflective practice on an interaction with an individual or community and specifically identifying: (1) What happened? (2) What does it mean? (3) What are the takeaways about how we think and act? (4) How would we approach a similar situation in the future? This exercise can be done independently via journaling and/or in discussion with a colleague, who may be able to offer additional insight from their outside perspective (Zettervall & Nienow, 2019). Most importantly, engaging in reflective practice exercises intended to increase self-awareness, such as the ones described, should be conducted routinely to develop and maintain one's sense of cultural humility, resulting in the ultimate goal of librarianship—compassionate, high-quality service for all patrons.

We should also take this process of growth one step further by educating ourselves about cultures that are different from our own. This has been described as cultural competency, but the word "competency" implies that there is an endpoint to learning about other cultures, meaning that we know everything there is to know about *other* cultures (Tucker, 2019). Preferably, the important part of this work is understanding that we will never be done with this exploration, and it is always our individual responsibility to continually learn about the people around us so we can foster stronger connections and provide better service.

Marginalization can be based on various factors, including race, ethnicity, gender, sexual orientation, disability, socioeconomic status, and more. Individuals from nonmarginalized groups need to engage in self-study to broaden their horizons rather than burdening people from marginalized groups with the physical and emotional labor of educating them and/or making them feel better about their ignorance. Nonmarginalized individuals can increase their knowledge in a number of ways:

- Reading independently or in groups, such as book clubs coordinated by the Medical Library Association (MLA) and the Association of Academic Health Sciences Libraries (AAHSL).
- Attending programming offered by affinity and identity groups within MLA and ALA or groups external to librarianship (e.g., the Association of American Medical Colleges).
- Viewing films and listening to podcasts that present the lived experiences of people who are different from themselves.
- Exposing themselves to the narratives of diverse groups by following librarians and other individuals who identify as Black, Indigenous, and People of Color (BIPOC) on social media (Hollis, 2018).

CULTURAL HUMILITY—INTERPERSONAL LEVEL

Shifting from the intrapersonal to the interpersonal level, the literature shows that libraries and librarians have investigated and considered how cultural humility can be applied to the work that they do with and for their users at the interpersonal level. The literature at this level can be viewed in three groups: (1) training for librarians to better understand and serve the communities in which they work, (2) resources librarians develop to help their patrons better understand cultural humility, and (3) enhanced practices that result in a collection inclusive of marginalized voices.

Building on the concept that cultural humility begins from within, some libraries have developed training programs for their staff that guide participants through internal reflection and group sharing. An activity designed by Ros Dorsman utilized bingo to engage librarians in discussions about variations in reading habits in different cultures, enabling them to practice communication and cultural humility about those differences (Dorsman, 2009). Another example described training volunteers for a free after-school Homework Help program in the Seattle Public Library system, where K–12 students from Seattle Public Schools could get help at their local public libraries. Prior to 2012, the volunteers teaching in this program were largely over fifty years old and predominantly white, whereas the children enrolled were largely from minority communities. In addition to making efforts to recruit a diverse pool of volunteers, the program provided training to engage tutors in the lifelong practice of learning about other cultures and strategies to hold themselves accountable for how cultural differences may affect teaching interactions. In essence, this is the practice of teaching cultural humility. The article about this example ended with a call to action and a road map for other libraries to implement this training in their own environment (Andrews et al., 2018). Overall, the work to increase cultural humility through training workshops for librarians is a growing enterprise and may inspire ideas for implementing similar programs in one's own workspace.

There has also been considerable work done around developing culturally aware information literacy education. The library literature includes research on how specific populations engage with the library and how their cultures may affect that interaction (Dorner & Gorman, 2006; Ghaddar & Caidi, 2014; Houlihan et al., 2017; Zhang & Lin, 2016). Houlihan et al. ended their investigation of how international students were utilizing library services with a challenge to librarians to learn about other cultures to foster cultural humility when serving patrons, regardless of their nation of origin. They also highlighted a need for cross-campus collaboration, which Stony Brook University took one step further (Houlihan et al., 2017). The library at Stony Brook recruited student members to their diversity committee to increase representation and develop programming that was authentically useful to their student population

(Ramonetti & Pilato, 2019). Stony Brook also pursued changes to their collection that embraced cultural humility and increased representation. The committee worked with the library's collections department to recommend the addition of oral histories to their collection. These histories brought additional perspectives and stories not otherwise covered in the collection (Ramonetti & Pilato, 2019).

There have been several specific examples of culturally aware collection development focusing on children's books (Cooper, 2005), music (Bartik, 2010), and e-books (Lear & Pritt, 2021). Birdi et al. (2012) delved deeper into the topic to investigate how items in their collection (in this case, fiction) that were classified based on the ethnicity of the author/subjects of the works were read by library patrons. While their results were at times contradictory, they highlighted the importance of including a wide variety of ethnic/cultural backgrounds in the fiction collection and that these works may be read beyond the culture in which they are written (Birdi et al., 2012). Broader collections have the potential to expand patrons' exposure to various cultures and assist them on their own cultural humility journeys.

Another approach to collections development that has gained momentum in recent years involves recruiting individuals from a particular ethnic group to collaborate with the library in curating the collection that caters to or represents the population it serves. This has been done in Canada with the Indigenous community (Ghaddar & Caidi, 2014). Herzinger and Patillo extend this practice by reflecting on who should have the power to create the archival material describing a cultural artifact. Should it be an "outsider" (e.g., the librarian-archivist in charge of the collection) or an individual describing his or her own work (Herzinger & Pattillo, 2021)? Engseth challenges archivists to engage in cultural competency as they are well-positioned to contribute to the discourse around equity in the library world and decisions for additions and removal of items in the collections they oversee (Engseth, 2018).

Overall, the scholarship at the interpersonal level in librarianship focuses on developing skills to serve all users individually, creating programs to engage and inform users, and curating collections that accurately and appropriately reflect the demographics of the institutions they serve and the communities they exist within. All three elements are needed to provide library users comprehensive and culturally sensitive services and resources.

CULTURAL HUMILITY—COLLECTIVE LEVEL

Individual self-reflection and interpersonal connection with folks from various backgrounds can contribute to developing more culturally sensitive collections and services for diverse audiences. Yet, ideally, we should be working toward diversifying the librarian profession, ensuring that our members more closely reflect the communities we serve. Table 5.1 shows the disparity between race

Table 5.1. Race of Librarians Compared with the General Population in the United States

	Librarians* (%)	General population** (%)
Race		
White	88.0	72.4
Black or African American	5.2	12.6
American Indian and Alaskan Native	<1.0	1.0
Asian/Pacific Islander	2.7	5.0
Two or more	0.8	2.9
Other race	n/a	6.2
Ethnicity		
Latino	3.1	16.4

*Librarians with MLIS or MA degree (American Library Association, 2012)
** 2010 census data; includes people reporting one race or two or more races (United States Census, 2011)

and ethnicity of credentialed librarians (i.e., with MLIS or MA degrees) as compared with the general population of the United States.

To make meaningful progress on increasing the diversity of the library and information science (LIS) profession, we need to engage in cultural humility at the collective level. Specifically, the profession needs to critically reflect on the current representation in librarianship and work to adjust the profession's system-level policies and practices. The goal of this work should be to ensure that library workplaces are genuinely welcoming to people from underrepresented communities. A place to start is by examining and ultimately letting go of the "vocational awe" that prohibits critique of the profession (Cheshire & Stout, 2020). "Vocational awe refers to the set of ideas, values, and assumptions librarians have about themselves and the profession that result in beliefs that libraries as institutions are inherently good and sacred, and therefore beyond critique" (Ettarh, 2018). This awe disproportionally promotes the nobility of the profession, leading some to view any efforts to modernize as attacks on the very institution of librarianship itself.

There is an opportunity for the LIS profession to rethink its position as a neutral entity within a political world and embrace the principles of social justice. Becoming actively anti-racist and supporting equal representation will allow libraries to provide equitable services and inclusive collections to historically disinvested communities that have been left out of so many spheres of American life, including libraries.

CRITICAL REFLECTION ON LACK OF RACIAL AND ETHNIC DIVERSITY IN THE LIS PROFESSION

This section first describes the conditions that limit the racial and ethnic diversity of the LIS profession, followed by meaningful suggestions for ways to include marginalized persons as professionals and users. The literature provides evidence of three key elements that contribute to the homogeneity of the LIS profession: (1) the high financial cost of entering the profession, (2) hiring practices, and (3) the negative and toxic work environment often experienced by minority groups in libraries.

Most professional librarian jobs require an MLIS from an ALA-accredited program, which entails a financial investment ranging from $9,000 to $74,000 and a minimum of one year (with a very heavy course load) to several years of study. In some cases, individuals employed in higher education can use a tuition benefit to obtain their degree at no cost. This is often limited in that an individual may only take a few credits or one to two classes per semester, requiring a longer time to degree completion (GetEducated.com, 2022). To ease this burden, Espinal suggests that library budgets should make positions accessible to those with undergraduate degrees and allocate funding for the MLIS degree for those employees (Espinal et al., 2021). In addition to the educational burden, most job postings require work experience in a library setting, which may involve unpaid or low-paying work (Gohr & Nova, 2020). Libraries could also expand the types of work experience required of job candidates, such as customer service in a retail setting or research in a nonacademic setting.

While lowering the barriers to entering the profession is necessary, it is not sufficient to increase diversity. Hiring practices also need to evolve. A Black librarian with an MLIS degree, ten years' experience working as a public-school teacher, and volunteer experience working in libraries reported submitting more than two hundred job applications over a period of more than three years to obtain her first job as a librarian (Matthews, 2018). A 2018 survey of U.S. library directors in the Southeast revealed that many libraries do not use appropriate hiring practices that would lead to greater diversity. Examples of appropriate hiring practices include structured interviewing, rubrics for evaluating candidates, collecting and analyzing job search data to assess the applicant pool's diversity, and informed placement of job ads for future open positions. Instead, many libraries continue to evaluate candidates using a subjective lens of "good fit," which includes getting along with team members and other vague terms such as "flexible" or "collegial." These practices result in perpetuating the dominance of white women in LIS, thus subverting attempts to diversify the profession (Cunningham et al., 2019). In addition, focusing on "good fit" may activate implicit biases, as individuals often prefer to associate with and feel an affinity for those who come from the same people group as they do.

Once librarians from marginalized groups get hired, they often experience the library workplace as a toxic environment. Alabi (2018) suggests evidence of this phenomenon can be found in the fact there are a variety of programs designed to support the entry of Black, Indigenous, and People of Color into librarianship including the following: the ALA Spectrum Scholarship Program, the Association of Research Libraries' Initiative to Recruit a Diverse Workforce, the Knowledge River Institute, and the Minnesota Institute for Early Career Librarians. However, the proportion of librarians of color has not increased significantly, which is likely due to the "revolving door cycle," meaning, a librarian of color is recruited into an organization, experiences a toxic work environment, and decides to resign. The toxic work environment may include microaggressions, requirements to participate in diversity committees (unlike their white counterparts), challenges to their expertise, and other indignities (Alabi, 2018).

Microaggressions are verbal comments or nonverbal gestures that convey subtle or indirect discrimination against members of marginalized groups (Harrison & Tanner, 2018). There are numerous examples in the literature of librarians experiencing microaggressions (Chou & Pho, 2018; Neely & López-McKnight, 2018). When encountering microaggressions, librarians from marginalized groups are tasked with the emotional labor of deciding how to address the situation: (1) "call out" the offender, (2) try to educate them and deal with potential defensiveness, or (3) just let it go since the fatigue of dealing with such comments is too great (Gohr & Nova, 2020). Silvia Lin Hanick, a Taiwanese American, describes her approach to dealing with microaggressions by distancing herself from her culture to fit into the library environment, such as laughing at jokes about her culture. Furthermore, she reports that she has hidden many aspects of her authentic self to assimilate and "make White people feel comfortable" in order to fit into the LIS profession (Hanick, 2018).

Librarians of color may also find that they are tasked with an increased service burden as compared to their white colleagues. Often, a librarian from an underrepresented community will be asked to serve on a diversity committee (Alabi, 2018) or create diversity programming in the library (Brown & Leung, 2018). This work is in addition to their regular duties and often does not receive the recognition it deserves for the amount of time the work takes from the librarian's primary responsibilities. This is true throughout academia but is exacerbated in librarianship because of the small percentage of librarians who are from minority groups. Librarians identifying as people of color also invest additional time and emotional labor in mentoring LIS students or new librarians of color since there are so few in the profession (Gohr & Nova, 2020). The lack of support, unequal service burden, and prevalent microaggressions in the library work environment led Leung to advise new people of color in libraries that they may need to consider leaving the profession due to perpetual "unhappiness" or lack of motivation (Leung, 2018).

CONCLUSION: FROM REFLECTION TO ACTION

Leveraging cultural humility at the communal level could increase the diversity of the profession and meaningfully serve historically disinvested communities. Critical reflection of the profession, like the discussion in this chapter, needs to occur across the library community. We *must* openly acknowledge our shortcomings and the toxicity of the library environment to minority communities so that we may effect meaningful change. As a profession, LIS must recognize that people of color are the experts on their experiences, and space, time, and attention must be provided to hear and showcase their narratives. LIS should also move away from the notion that "all viewpoints [are] equal and valid, including viewpoints that compromise the safety of [people of color] POC" (Chiu et al., 2021, 63). "We cannot be equally accommodating to vicious racist beliefs and to patrons of color" (Cheshire & Stout, 2020).

This revolution needs to begin at the top with senior leaders of the LIS profession and libraries being the forerunners of cultural change in the profession. Individuals from marginalized groups must be embraced in positions of power, so they can be authentic and valued leaders in the conversation about how to change the environment (Brown & Leung, 2018). For example, as university librarian of the University of North Carolina at Chapel Hill (UNC CH), Elaine Westbrooks spearheaded a racial reckoning initiative. She supported the creation of a grant program with $250,000 for "allocating resources to library staff focused on initiating and advancing social justice and anti-racist work in and for the libraries" (Figueroa & Shawgo, 2022, 30–31). Projects funded under this initiative included (a) the development of transcription practices to make oral histories equitable and (b) the creation of inclusive and accessible guidelines for the description of special collections materials. In addition, the Inclusion, Diversity, Equity, and Accessibility (IDEA) Council at the University Libraries of UNC CH shepherded the creation of individual and department-level performance goals related to inclusion within the unit (Figueroa & Shawgo, 2022). Such performance goals are critical to acknowledging diversity and inclusion work as central to the mission of libraries and driving the cultural change needed to make libraries inclusive of all.

Real cultural change does not happen overnight; rather, it requires months and years of focused action. We hope the information provided in this chapter to support cultural humility practice at the intrapersonal, interpersonal, and communal levels fosters the changes needed to help libraries evolve into institutions that embrace justice and authentically represent and respect the people they serve.

REFERENCES

Alabi, J. (2018). From hostile to inclusive: Strategies for improving the racial climate of academic libraries. *Library Trends, 67*(1), 131–146. https://doi.org/10.1353/lib.2018.0029

American Library Association. (2006a, June 30). *Libraries: An American value* [Text]. Advocacy, Legislation & Issues. https://www.ala.org/advocacy/intfreedom/americanvalue

American Library Association. (2006b, June 30). *Library Bill of Rights* [Text]. Advocacy, Legislation & Issues. https://www.ala.org/advocacy/intfreedom/librarybill

American Library Association. (2012). *Diversity Counts 2009–2010 update.* https: https://www.ala.org/aboutala/offices/diversity/diversitycounts/2009-2010update

Andrews, N., Kim, S., & Watanabe, J. (2018). Cultural humility as a transformative framework for librarians, tutors, and youth volunteers: Applying a lens of cultural responsiveness in training library staff and volunteers. *Young Adult Library Services, 16*(2), 19–22. lii.

Bartik, E. L. (2010). World music, education, and the public library. *Music Reference Services Quarterly, 13*(3/4), 112–115. lxh.

Birdi, B., Wilson, K., & Mansoor, S. (2012). "What we should strive for is Britishness": An attitudinal investigation of ethnic diversity and the public library. *Journal of Librarianship & Information Science, 44*(2), 118–128. lxh.

Brown, J. & Leung, S. (2018). Authenticity vs. professionalism: Being true to ourselves at work. In R. L. Chou & A. Pho (eds.), *Pushing the margins: Women of color and intersectionality in LIS* (pp. 329–348). Library Juice Press.

Cheshire, K., & Stout, J. (2020). The moral arc of the library: What are our duties and limitations after 45? *Reference Services Review, 48*(2), 219–225. https://doi.org/10.1108/RSR-10-2019-0074

Chiu, A., Ettarh, F. M., & Ferretti, J. A. (2021). Not the shark, but the water: How neutrality and vocational awe intertwine to uphold white supremacy. In S. Y. Leung & J. R. López-McKnight (eds.), *Knowledge justice: Disrupting library and information studies through critical race theory*, 49–71. The MIT Press. https://doi.org/10.7551/mitpress/11969.003.0005

Chou, R. L., & Pho, A. (2018). *Pushing the margins: Women of color and intersectionality in LIS.* Library Juice Press.

Chowdhury, G., Poulter, A., & McMenemy, D. (2006). Public Library 2.0: Towards a new mission for public libraries as a "network of community knowledge." *Online Information Review, 30*(4), 454–460. https://doi.org/10.1108/14684520610686328

Cooper, S. (2005). Only the rarest kind of best: One view of literary criticism. *Children & Libraries: The Journal of the Association for Library Service to Children, 3*(2), 14–17. lxh.

Cunningham, S., Guss, S., & Stout, J. (2019). Challenging the "good fit" narrative: Creating inclusive recruitment practices in academic libraries. *Recasting the Narrative: The Proceedings of the ACRL 2019 Conference, April 10–13, 2019, Cleveland, Ohio,* 12–21.

Dorner, D. G., & Gorman, G. E. (2006). Information literacy education in Asian developing countries: Cultural factors affecting curriculum development and programme delivery. *Ausbildung Der Informationskompetenz in Den Entwicklungsländern Asiens: Kulturelle Faktoren, Die Die Ausarbeitung Der*

Bildungspläne Und Der Vorgelegten Programme Beeinflussen, 32(4), 281–293. lxh.

Dorsman, R. (2009). Reading bingo! *InCite: Newsletter of the Australian Library and Information Association, 30*(6), 18. lxh.

Engseth, E. (2018). Cultural competency: A framework for equity, diversity, and inclusion in the archival profession in the United States. *American Archivist, 81*(2), 460–482. lxh.

Espinal, I., Hathcock, A. M., & Rios, M. (2021). Dewhitening librarianship: A policy proposal for libraries. In S. Y. Leung & J. R. López-McKnight (eds.), *Knowledge justice: Disrupting library and information studies through critical race theory* (pp. 223–240). The MIT Press. https://doi.org/10.7551/mitpress/11969.001.0001

Ettarh, Fobazi. (2018). Vocational awe and librarianship: The lies we tell ourselves. In the Library with the Lead Pipe. https://www.inthelibrarywiththeleadpipe.org/2018/vacationalawe/

Figueroa, M., & Shawgo, K. (2022). "You can't read your way out of racism": Creating anti-racist action out of education in an academic library. *Reference Services Review, 50*(1), 25–39. lxh.

GetEducated.com. (2022). *The 40 most affordable master's in library science online.* GetEducated: Review, Rate, Rank & Compare Online Colleges & Degrees. https://www.geteducated.com/online-college-ratings-and-rankings/best-buy-lists/affordable-online-library-science-masters-degrees/

Ghaddar, J., & Caidi, N. (2014). Indigenous knowledge in a post-apology era: Steps toward healing and bridge building. *Bulletin of the Association for Information Science & Technology, 40*(5), 41–45. lxh.

Gohr, M., & Nova, V. A. (2020). Student trauma experiences, library instruction and existence under the 45th. *Reference Services Review, 48*(1), 183–199. lxh.

Hanick, Silvia Lin. (2018). "The shoe is too small and not made for you!": Racial "covering" and the illusion of fit. In T. Y. Neely & J. R. López-McKnight (eds.), *In our own voices, redux: The faces of librarianship today* (pp. 83–92). Rowman & Littlefield.

Harrison, C., & Tanner, K. D. (2018). Language matters: considering microaggressions in science. *CBE Life Sciences Education, 17*(1), fe4. https://doi.org/10.1187/cbe.18-01-0011. Erratum in: *CBE Life Sciences Education, 19*(4), co2. (2020, December).

Haynes-Mendez, K., & Engelsmeier, J. (2020). Cultivating cultural humility in education. *Childhood Education, 96*(3), 22–29. https://doi.org/10.1080/00094056.2020.1766656

Herzinger, K., & Pattillo, R. (2021, September 15). *Reflections on active collecting during difficult times.* In the Library with the Lead Pipe. https://www.inthelibrarywiththeleadpipe.org/2021/active-collecting/

Hodge, T. (2019). Integrating cultural humility into public services librarianship. *International Information & Library Review, 51*(3), 268–274. lii.

Hollis, D. R. (2018). Still ambiguous after all these years: Reflections on diversity in academic libraries. In T. Y. Neely & J. R. López-McKnight (eds.), *In our own voices, redux: The faces of librarianship today* (pp. 3–11). Rowman & Littlefield.

Houlihan, M., Walker Wiley, C., & Click, A. B. (2017). International students and information literacy: A systematic review. *Reference Services Review, 45*(2), 258–277. lxh.

Hughes, V., Delva, S., Nkimbeng, M., Spaulding, E., Turkson-Ocran, R.-A., Cudjoe, J., Ford, A., Rushton, C., D'Aoust, R., & Han, H.-R. (2020). Not missing the opportunity: Strategies to promote cultural humility among future nursing faculty. *Journal of Professional Nursing: Official Journal of the American Association of Colleges of Nursing, 36*(1), 28–33. https://doi.org/10.1016/j.profnurs.2019.06.005

Kangos, K. A., & Pieterse, A. L. (2021). Examining how lesbian, gay, and bisexual Christian clients' perceptions of therapists' cultural humility contribute to psychotherapy outcomes. *Psychotherapy (Chicago, Ill.), 58*(2), 254–262. https://doi.org/10.1037/pst0000375

Lear, B. A., & Pritt, A. L. (2021). "We need diverse e-books": Availability of award-winning children's and young adult titles in today's e-book platforms. *Collection Management, 46*(3/4), 223–247. lxh.

Lekas, H.-M., Pahl, K., & Fuller Lewis, C. (2020). Rethinking cultural competence: Shifting to cultural humility. *Health Services Insights, 13*, 1178632920970580. https://doi.org/10.1177/1178632920970580

Leung, Sofia. (2018). Letter to new people of color in LIS. In T. Y. Neely & J. R. López-McKnight (eds.), *In our own voices, redux: The faces of librarianship today* (pp. 257–264). Rowman & Littlefield.

Matthews, Leni. (2018). Grief in five stages: Post-graduate librarian degree. In T. Y. Neely & J. R. López-McKnight (eds.), *In our own voices, redux: The faces of librarianship today* (pp. 165–172). Rowman & Littlefield.

Neely, T. Y., & López-McKnight, J. R. (2018). *In our own voices, redux: The faces of librarianship today*. Rowman & Littlefield.

Project Implicit. (2011). *Take a test*. https://implicit.harvard.edu/implicit/takeatest.html

Ramonetti, M., & Pilato, V. (2019). Keeping the equity, inclusion, and diversity conversations Going. *Urban Library Journal, 25*(1), 1–15. lxh.

Tervalon, M., & Murray-Garcia, J. (1998). Cultural humility versus cultural competence: A critical distinction in defining physician training outcomes in multicultural education. *Journal of Health Care for the Poor and Underserved, 9*(2), 117–125. https://doi.org/10.1353/hpu.2010.0233

Tucker, A. F. (2019). Cultural issues in the consumer health library. *Journal of Hospital Librarianship, 19*(4), 339–344.

United States Census. (2011). *Race and Hispanic origin and the 2010 Census*. https://www.census.gov/data/tables/2023/dec/2020-dhc-hispanic-pop-supplemental-table.html.

Wood, E. (2021). Libraries rull circle: The cross section of community, the public sphere, and third place. *Public Library Quarterly, 40*(2), 144–166. https://doi.org/10.1080/01616846.2020.1737491

Zettervall, S., & Nienow, M. C. (2019). *Sustainable practice*. Libraries Unlimited.

Zhang, Y., & Lin, Y.-H. (2016). Writing a Wikipedia article on cultural competence in health care. *Medical Reference Services Quarterly, 35*(2), 175–186.

6

Exploring Identities to Improve Library Practice

Andrea Hayes and Tamara M. Nelson

Identity is "the fact of being who or what a person or thing is" (Oxford Languages, 2022). It includes those characteristics we ascribe to and those ascribed to us. Understanding our identity is critical to practicing cultural humility, as we must first understand ourselves to understand others. This chapter will provide practical resources for understanding your own identity and that of others. Library practice can be positively impacted if we know not only our own cultural identity but that of our colleagues and the patrons we serve.

How do you begin to explore your identity? First, start by recognizing that it is not only about positive traits but can also involve acknowledging negative traits. Regarding cultural identity, characteristics include gender, race, history, nationality, language, sexuality, religion, ethnicity, aesthetics, disabilities, and even the food you eat. Your identity is fluid and can be influenced by social awareness, education, experience, and exposure. It is essential to be aware of the fluidity of identity as we interact with our colleagues and patrons.

Social identity groups are based on individuals' physical, social, and mental characteristics. These characteristics may not always be prominent and can be self-claimed or ascribed. For example, racial identity can be based on the individual's assertion or belief (self-proclaimed) or assigned to individuals by society without their active choice or effort (ascribed). Sexual orientation, religion, and disability status can be personally claimed but may not often be visible. It is also important to note that conflict often arises in the terms used to describe social identity when individuals choose to self-identify as something society feels they are not. Therefore, it is critical to recognize the importance of an individual's right to self-identify. In other words, we define who we are on our terms.

There have been many exercises developed to help in the process of defining identity. These exercises are often used in secondary and higher education as students explore their identity and how to explain it. In a practice developed for the University of Michigan Inclusive Teaching, author Pabdoo (n.d.) walks students through exploring their social identity using the Social Identity Wheel. The exercise aims "to encourage students to reflect on the relationships and dissonances between their personal and social identities" (Pabdoo, n.d.). Though the publication date of this source is unknown, Figure 6.1 provides a list of frequently used identities to aid in exploring your identity.

Though this list is a good starting point for exploring identity, the terms could be more inclusive. Consequently, individuals may select words that are not included but best represent their identity while refraining from choices that could be deemed offensive. According to the Ontario Human Rights Commission (n.d.), gender identity is an individual's internal and personal experience of gender. It is a person's sense of being a woman, man, both, or neither. It may also be the same or different from a person's assigned sex at birth. The Guide

Gender	man, woman, transgender, gender neutral, non-binary, agender, pangender, genderqueer, etc.
Sex	Intersex, female, male
Race	Asian Pacific Islander, Native American, Latinx, Black, White, Bi/Multiracial
Sexual Orientation	Lesbian, Gay, Bisexual, Pan-Attractional, Heterosexual, Queer, Attractionality, Questioning
Religion/Spirituality	Hindu, Muslim, Buddhist, Jewish, Christian, Pagan, Agnostic, Faith/Meaning, Atheist, Secular Humanist
Social Class	Poor, Working Class, Lower-Middle Class, Upper-Middle Class, Owning Class, Ruling Class
Age	Child, Young Adult, Middle-Age Adult, Senior
(Dis)Ability	People with disabilities (cognitive, physical, emotional, etc.), Temporarily able-bodied, Temporarily disabled
Nation(s) of Origin and/or Citizenship	United States, Nigeria, Korea, Turkey, Argentina
Tribal or Indigenous Affiliation	Mohawk, Aboriginal, Navajo, Santal
Body Size/ Type	Fat, Person of Size, Thin

Figure 6.1. Definitions of Identity Types.

to Gender Identity Terms (Wamsley, 2021), a glossary of terms to define gender and identity, is summarized below. Understanding these terms is necessary for cultural humility because gender identity is often misunderstood.

Sex refers to a person's biological status and is typically assigned at birth based on external anatomy. Sex is typically categorized as male, female, or intersex.

Gender is often defined as a social construct of norms, behaviors, and roles that varies between societies and over time. Gender is often categorized as male, female, or nonbinary.

Gender identity is one's internal sense of self and gender, whether that is man, woman, neither, or both. Unlike gender expression, gender identity is not necessarily outwardly visible to others.

Gender expression is how a person presents gender outwardly through behavior, clothing, voice, or other perceived characteristics. Society identifies these cues as masculine or feminine, although what is considered masculine or feminine changes over time and varies by culture.

Cisgender, often abbreviated as "cis," describes a person whose gender identity aligns with the sex they were assigned at birth.

Transgender, often abbreviated as "trans," describes someone whose gender identity differs from the sex assigned at birth. A transgender man, for example, is someone who was listed as female at birth but whose gender identity is male.

Nonbinary is a term that can be used by people who do not describe themselves or their genders as fitting into the categories of man or woman. A range of terms is used to refer to these experiences, and "nonbinary" and "genderqueer" are among those that are sometimes used.

Agender can describe a person who does not identify as any gender.

Gender-expansive can describe someone with a more flexible gender identity than might be associated with a typical gender binary.

Gender transition is a process a person may take to bring themselves and/or their bodies into alignment with their gender identity. Transitioning is not just one step and can include any, none, or all the following: telling one's friends, family, and coworkers; changing one's name and pronouns; updating legal documents; going through medical interventions like hormone therapy or undergoing a surgical intervention, often referred to as gender confirmation surgery.

Gender dysphoria refers to psychological distress that results from an incongruence between one's sex assigned at birth and one's gender identity. Though this can affect individuals of various gender identities, not all people experience it, and those who may can encounter it at varying intensity levels.

Sexual orientation refers to the enduring physical, romantic, and/or emotional attraction to members of the same and/or other genders, including lesbian, gay, bisexual, and heterosexual orientations.

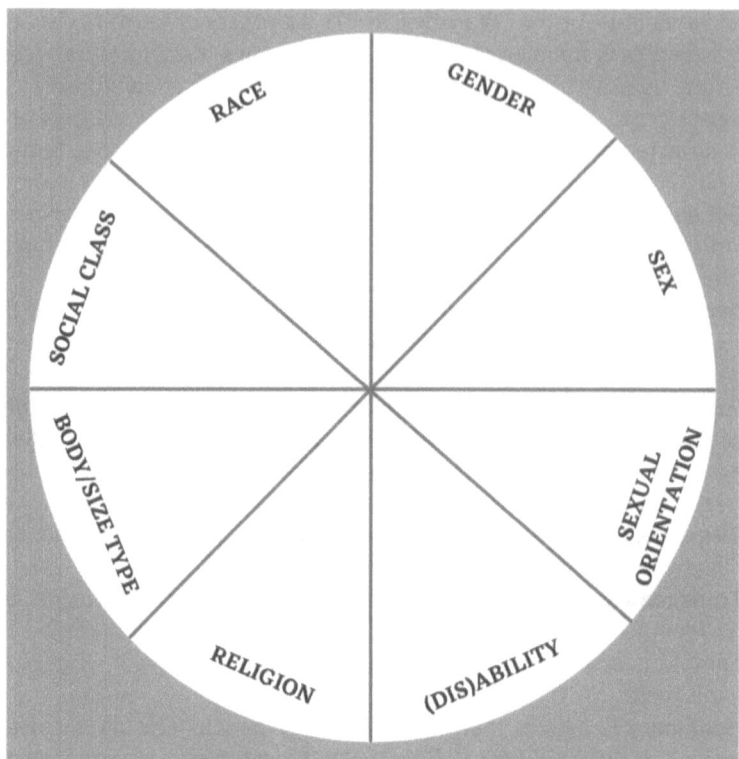

Figure 6.2. Understanding Your Identity *Adapted by the authors from the Social Identity Wheel (Pabdoo, n.d.).*

Intersex is an umbrella term used to describe people with differences in reproductive anatomy, chromosomes, or hormones that do not fit typical definitions of male and female.

Other important terms when considering social identity groups include: (1) **marginalized**—those who are disenfranchised or exploited, and (2) **privileged**—those who hold unearned advantages in society. Individuals may be assigned and/or identified as members of either group. (Wamsley, 2021)

DEFINING SOCIAL IDENTITY

Often when we work with others, we fail to fully consider that they, too, are more than just their immediate roles, like Sharon, the librarian who manages the circulation desk. The people with whom we work are, in fact, individuals with lives, families, homes, pets, and sometimes even illnesses that they carry to and from the workplace each day. All these things, these pieces of self, are building blocks that make up our identities, which many say makes us who we are.

In social identity theory, "how people come to see themselves as members of one group/category" (Stets & Burke, 2000, 226) provides most people with feelings of self-worth and a sense of self-identity. This also means that as a global community, we can easily categorize others and ourselves. For example, as one of the authors of this chapter, I am a young African American woman and a scholar. I am Southern and have a chronic illness. All these things combine to make up my social identity. I use these factors of self to determine whom I can easily relate to in my day-to-day life, my workplace, and other facets of living.

One's social identity is rooted in who they are and how they present themselves when meeting others. Characteristic of social identity theory, there are "in-groups" and "out-groups" and "persons who are similar ... are labeled in the in-group; persons who differ ... are categorized as the out-group" (Stets & Burke, 2000, 225). This is pivotal for social development within and outside of ourselves. Once we have developed who we are and determined what groups we belong to, some of which we have control over (occupation, religion), and some we do not (ethnicity, nationality), it raises the question about what it means for ourselves, those around us, and our libraries.

Essentially, it means that we go about our lives, associating with those we determine are in our "in-groups" and sometimes avoiding those we determine are in our "out-groups." Ultimately, we make friends and colleagues, develop relationships in various aspects of our lives, and become functioning human beings. This is true for every part of our life—work, social, familial, etc. So, when we think about our lives in the library, we must consider that, as social beings, we will connect with our colleagues and patrons daily. Our unique social identities unite to create a global community that shapes our distinctive library space. These library spaces can be comfortable or uncomfortable for our colleagues, patrons, and ourselves. It is up to each of us to determine the cohesiveness and safety of our spaces.

The notion of stereotyping is another part of social identity theory that is important to note. In Henri Tajfel's original approach, the idea of categorizing one another into groups of "us" vs. "them" was based on a "normal cognitive process" (McLeod, 2019), in other words, it is something that people tend to do, no matter how "right" or "wrong" others feel it may be. Stereotyping is expected today, and as a result, many of our identities are wrapped up in versions of stereotypes that people often believe. For example, when I tell people I am from southwest Georgia, they think I will have a deep Southern drawl when I speak because I hail from the Deep South. Another version of that stereotype is that people assume I come from Atlanta (which I do not). Stereotypes are not always steeped in truth but are sometimes engrossed in misconceptions.

WHAT DOES ALL OF THIS MEAN FOR LIBRARIES AND LIBRARY PRACTICE?

When we interact with one another in our day-to-day lives, it is important not to assume or stereotype. Each of our identities is vastly different, making each of us unique. Those unique differences, in turn, give rise to many experiences at our libraries. At the foundation, however, we are all librarians. This common denominator can ultimately bring us together.

We may all be in the same "in-group" as librarians. Many of us began this profession with the primary purpose and objective of serving others and imparting knowledge. Though many ventured into technical services, reference, research, education, interlibrary loan, and other areas, the core goal of educating and assisting others has remained constant, but within that are our identities.

How we interact within our various departments or during university or departmental social gatherings may impact our workplace environment and influence how we perceive our colleagues in subsequent interactions. Consider the following scenario as an example. You have started at your new library and are excited to meet your new colleagues and begin work. You identify as an African American woman (AAW). When someone who identifies as a white woman (WW) sees you in the hallway standing between an elevator and a trash can, they make an assumption. The conversation proceeds like this:

WW: "Hello, are you here to pick up my trash?"
AAW: "I'm sorry?"
WW: "You there. You must be here to get my trash."
AAW: "Um, no. I'm new here. I'm a faculty member."

The above interaction could have severe ramifications for either woman. The AAW, for example, would be hurt for not being recognized as a colleague and for the microaggression and inherent racism. A lousy work encounter has now tarnished her self-identity. Once the implicit bias is brought to the attention of the WW, she might likely experience embarrassment and remorse, or she may avoid, deny, or defend her behavior.

WHAT ABOUT INTERACTIONS AFTER THE FACT?

Our interactions are based mainly on our identities or how we perceive ourselves and others. Thus, when we interact with others, those perceptions, in a sense, *bleed* into conversations and nonverbal communication, like facial expressions. Discussing our social identities raises a crucial question: How do we want our connections with colleagues and patrons to make us feel?

Consider another sample scenario and possible interaction: a faculty member (Annie) has an invisible illness that was revealed by another colleague (without Annie's knowledge) to her department head (Kim).

Annie: Hi, Kim. How are you today?
Kim: Hi, Annie. Can you come to see me for a moment?
Annie: Sure.
Kim: I hear you have endometriosis. Will this affect your work in any way?
Annie: No, not at all. My chronic illness is managed quite well.
Kim: All right.

The primary issue is that this conversation is inappropriate since Annie was unaware Kim knew about her illness. Another colleague, whom Annie had confided in, revealed this information to her department head.

Considering the interaction that did take place in this scenario, both women are likely feeling very uneasy. Kim did not ease into the subject with Annie, and Annie did not have an opportunity to prepare for the conversation in any way. Kim's apparent bias in this situation is that Annie's chronic illness will render her work less than optimal. If Annie was experiencing performance issues, then a private discussion to explore potential accommodations that could assist her would have been more appropriate in this situation.

Let us revisit the women after department head Kim has had time to rethink the initial conversation.

Kim: Hi, Annie; I wanted to apologize for my earlier assumption about your health. Please let me know how I can help you in any way.
Annie: Thank you, Kim. I appreciate that.

Here we see a small exchange with significant results. Kim likely realized that assuming Annie's work performance would not be adequate due to her chronic illness was a biased stereotype. By assuming someone who is not equally abled cannot do something as well as someone who is, we are automatically setting a bar of bias and restricting humility in the workplace. Instead, we want to be sure we are creating an atmosphere of tolerance, understanding, and cultural humility.

CONCLUSION

Maya Angelou is credited with saying, "I've learned that people will forget what you said, people will forget what you did, but people will never forget how you made them feel." In many ways, what Angelou said is true. After time has passed, we may not remember the exact phrasing of someone's words or actions, but we will not forget how those words and actions made us feel. Moreover, this is important regarding our daily social interactions. Every one of us possesses a vastly different identity. These differences make us all individuals, bringing uniqueness to our libraries.

REFERENCES

McLeod, S. A. (2019, October 24.). *Social identity theory.* Simply Psychology. www.simplypsychology.org/social-identity-theory.html

Ontario Human Rights Commission. (n.d.). *Gender identity and gender expression.* https://www.ohrc.on.ca/en/policy-preventing-discrimination-because-gender-identity-and-gender-expression/3-gender-identity-and-gender-expression#:~:text=Gender%20identity%20is%20each%20person's,from%20their%20birth%2Dassigned%20sex

Oxford Languages. (2022). Oxford University Press.

Pabdoo. (n.d.). *Social identity wheel.* Inclusive Teaching. https://sites.lsa.umich.edu/inclusive-teaching/social-identity-wheel/

Stets, J. E. and Burke, P. J. (2000). Identity theory and social identity theory. *Social Psychology Quarterly, 63*(3), 224–237.

Wamsley, L. (2021). *A guide to gender identity terms.* National Public Radio. https://www.npr.org/2021/06/02/996319297/gender-identity-pronouns-expression-guide-lgbtq

7

Advancing Cultural Humility in Dental Education

Irene M. Lubker and Joni Nelson

In this chapter, we discuss strategies and offer perspectives for advancing cultural humility in the health sciences, focusing on predoctoral dental education and research, our niche area. Foundationally, dental education has taken many strides to increase diversity, and both authors identify as Black women in this field. In 2016, the American Dental Education Association conducted a study to define the state of racial, ethnic diversity, and gender in dental education (Cook, 2016). The study also differentiated data critical for identifying challenges to increasing diversity, including the distribution of nonwhites (i.e., Native Americans, Asians, Hispanics, African Americans) and whites among multiple health professional training programs. The combined percentages of nonwhite graduates of these health professions included: pharmacy, 35 percent; dentistry, 33 percent; medicine 32 percent; osteopathic medicine, 26 percent; law school 25 percent; and veterinary medicine 13 percent. Therefore, the gap in racial distribution presents an opportunity to create an environment that espouses cultural humility within the dental training setting, which is critical for optimal dental health-care outcomes.

Definitions of "cultural humility" place emphasis on the continuum of the process "that incorporates a lifelong commitment to self-evaluation and critique, to redressing the power imbalances in the physician-patient dynamic, and to developing mutually beneficial and non-paternalistic partnerships with communities on behalf of individuals and defined populations," which means taking a non-superior stance when confronted with a different culture and going further by regarding the differences as positive additions (Tervalon & Murray-Garcia, 1998). Embracing diverse cultures can enable you to become aware of those different from your own, thereby moving you slowly toward cultural humility. Solchanyk et al. (2021) stated it best when they referred to cultural humility as a dynamic process with social justice goals, requiring continuous hard work, respect, understanding of other cultures, and flexibility. Furthermore, cultural humility expands on cultural competence as it focuses on openness to aspects of cultural identity most important to the patient (Trinh, 2021) Practicing cultural humility can shed light on issues that could hinder quality health-care delivery, thereby improving patient care and openness.

We recognize that cultural humility cannot be separated from the provision of patient care, especially in dentist-patient communication. This is the backbone for optimal oral health outcomes and a necessity for predoctoral dental training activities and classroom engagement. As dental educators, we strive to produce future dentists who are continually working toward delivering quality dental-care services with cultural humility. Fortunately, the American Dental Education Association (ADEA), "the voice of dental education," recognizes the importance of "driving strategic planning in the areas of diversity and cultural competency; furthering the dialogue around inclusive environments." The ADEA Access, Diversity and Inclusion Strategic Framework helps to guide incorporation of diversity and inclusion in dental education (American Dental Education Association, 2020). The National Standards for Culturally and Linguistically Appropriate Services (CLAS) in Health and Health Care are also available to "promote and advance health equity, improve quality, and help eliminate health care disparities by providing effective, equitable, understandable, and respectful quality care and services that are responsive to diverse cultural health beliefs and practices, preferred languages, health literacy, and other communication needs" (U.S. Department of Health and Human Resources—Office of Minority Health, 2013). By regularly incorporating these tools into dental education, we can prioritize the two frameworks into actionable dental medicine curricula competencies.

Some dental colleges have classes or programs geared toward teaching cultural humility, and others have invited instruction by librarians who use various methods to teach cultural competence and humility. Librarians are positioned to integrate cultural humility in their instruction and other areas of librarianship (Hodge, 2019). Goodman and Nugent (2020) described their experiences teaching cultural competence and cultural humility to predoctoral dental students at the University of Nevada's School of Dental Medicine using storytelling, interaction, and critical-thinking dialogue. At the Medical University of South Carolina, a cultural competence program was inserted into the curricula with the first- and second-year predoctoral students (Pilcher et al., 2008). The program has since expanded to all four years of the dental school curricula.

In this chapter, we will discuss some of our institution's efforts to elevate cultural humility in our students, staff, and faculty in the dental college. These efforts align with the university-wide strategic plan and dental accreditation competencies (Commission on Dental Accreditation, 2020; MUSC James B. Edwards College of Dental Medicine Dental Faculty Meeting, 2020; MUSC Office of Diversity and Inclusion, 2022; Office of Diversity for the MUSC James B. Edwards College of Dental Medicine, 2022). We hope the strategies for our dental college will work with other health sciences programs such as nursing, medical, pharmacy, and allied health sciences at other institutions.

INTRODUCING CULTURAL HUMILITY INTO THE DENTAL CURRICULA: PERSPECTIVES FROM THE FIELD

A variety of efforts have been made in our dental college to support students, staff, and faculty for the elevation of cultural humility. The approach of these endeavors is in alignment with a university-wide strategic plan, dental program accreditation competencies, and college-specific goals (Commission on Dental Accreditation, 2020; MUSC James B. College of Dental Medicine Dental Faculty Meeting, 2020; MUSC Office of Diversity and Inclusion, 2022; Office of Diversity for the MUSC James B. Edwards College of Dental Medicine, 2022). In this regard, we are going to highlight three exemplary areas where our college has successfully established strategies for integrating cultural humility within training for predoctoral dental students.

The first area of prioritization for cultural humility, professional development and advancement, trends across all staff, faculty, and students in a collective action approach to strengthen competence levels of cultural humility among all members within our college. Examples include on-campus diversity and inclusion seminars, enterprise-wide required equity training, and college-specific workshops. Our campus offers many in-person and virtual seminars for diversity, equity, and inclusion that prioritize the learner's ability to acquire and apply culturally responsive strategies in their delivery of health-care services, research initiatives, and teaching efforts. As part of our institution's goal to nurture an inclusive environment and experience for all the lives we touch, a four-hour annual diversity, equity, and inclusion training is required for all employees and students across the institutional enterprise. This intentional effort to calibrate all members within our institution creates a foundational standard for our predoctoral dental students to adapt beyond their current training into their future professional dental careers. Additionally, our college hosts dental-specific workshops emphasizing the significance of cultural humility in our clinical, research, and didactic settings. One of the more notable workshops, led by librarians Irene Lubker and Amanda Nevius, focused on anti-racism and was intended to increase cultural humility by inciting awareness and stimulating discussion among participants (i.e., students and faculty) regarding health equity and evidence-based practice to improve their cultural humility. The workshop began by showing the participants the library guide of anti-racism resources, followed by summaries of four papers discussing health disparities and racism in dentistry. Participants were then divided into smaller groups and given articles to discuss about the content and actions they would take considering the discussion. Participants then returned to the larger group to give their reports and ask questions. One of the articles discussed in the workshop was about orthodontic standards that were used across all patients without recognizing the differences in natural facial profiles (Sushner, 1977). The questions and comments indicated that engaging with the anti-racism and health equity literature enabled the participants to become more empathetic to issues that minority groups experience. Both the LibGuide and the virtual anti-racism workshop are tools for climbing the cultural humility ladder to decrease biases and improve clinical outcomes.

The second area of prioritization for cultural humility is specialized courses and mentorship for students. In this area, our college has excelled in developing and delivering courses that prepare predoctoral dental students by fostering a learning environment for delivering humanistic care among a diverse patient population. Predoctoral dental students have access to multifaceted courses with tenets of cultural humility. Specifically, we will highlight two elective courses focusing on elevating their knowledge and application of (1) interprofessional oral health-care delivery for individuals with special health-care needs and (2) patient management and empathetic care for underserved populations. The "Special Teams—Interprofessional Rotation" elective course aims to improve oral and systemic health-care outcomes for patients with special health-care needs (SHCN). Predoctoral dental students also advance their practice of cultural humility by their engagement with patients and their families. Their rotation experience also supports a team-based learning approach composed of dental, occupational therapy, pharmacy, and physician assistant students to enhance their interprofessional competencies in the clinical care of adults with SHCN. Student teams discuss current medical and dental health medications, including possible side effects and oral sequelae. Discussions about preventive medical and oral health care are also held with patients and their families or caretakers to increase their understanding of issues involved in caring for adults with SHCN. The second elective course, "Impacts of Poverty and Healthcare Consumerism," addresses the determinants of health as it relates to health-care consumerism and health status trajectories for the U.S. population living in poverty. The motivation for this course is not to be delivered as a theoretical didactic but as a skill-building course to cultivate cultural humility and empathy for patients who do not have a shared lived experience with their provider. The course is asynchronous, online, and organized into two sections: fundamentals of poverty and health and reducing risks through clinical practice.

The students also have access to mentorship through two college-specific programs, MINTS (Mentoring Is Navigating Together Strongly) and the Safety Net Dental Club. The MINTS project is the result of our college's effort to provide mini awards to faculty addressing the goals of our current strategic plan. It was designed to develop a mentoring model for underrepresented, minority dental students to facilitate successful matriculation with support during dental school. The program has also nurtured an environment for dialogue among mentees regarding cultural competence, trust, and respect for differences in their mentee-mentor relationships, and responsiveness to a diverse dental health-care team. To address student demand for training on health services research methodologies, including policies and practices that govern the safety net, we established the Safety Net Dental Research and Journal Club. To bridge and ameliorate the care gaps between research and translation into practice, this forum applies methodologies that focus on evidence-based, culturally responsive care for rural and economically disadvantaged communities. The group meets for an hour every other month for a minimum of four student contact hours. Topics of discussion have included: public policies that shape utilization behaviors of rural and/or economically disadvantaged patients, research skill development framed by culturally sensitive approaches unique to the target population, a "day in the life" of a safety net provider, provider testimony on behalf of their patients, and techniques for establishing self-management goals with patients.

The final area of prioritization for cultural humility in our college is library resources to empower faculty and students to learn more about diverse cultures. One way of achieving this is for the librarians to showcase accessible resources that teach the experiences of minority groups and embrace the literature of race. We have developed a guide with a collection of resources that highlight the convergence between racism and dentistry/oral health to facilitate anti-racism awareness and encourage discussion in the classroom and the workplace. Additionally, a collection of articles, e-books, and videos on health disparity and its correlation with racism are freely available through the library. More specifically, we have shared a video by Amanda Nevius that explains why it is necessary to have both the American Dental Association and the National Dental Association. It should also be noted that the orthodontic paper discussed at the previously mentioned anti-racism workshop came from Howard University, one of the only two historically Black universities with predoctoral dental programs. These critical examples of library resources remind us of the value of incorporating marginalized voices to help elevate cultural humility within dental curricula and education.

Library orientation and evidence-based dentistry classes provide natural opportunities to be inclusive of cultural humility development. During these sessions, librarians discuss the importance of cultural humility in oral care to introduce first-year predoctoral dental students to the importance of shifting their personal perspectives, continually focusing on the experiences and needs of their patients from other cultures, and addressing differences with positive attitudes (Venditto & Colón, 2022). In the evidence-based dentistry course, the librarian utilizes the Association of College and Research Libraries (ACRL) framework for information literacy to prioritize cultural humility by discussing the ACRL frame, "Information Has Value." Students learn that the value of information can be distorted by systemic policies and discrimination, resulting in the marginalization of minority voices. Students are also instructed to recognize that intellectual property is a legal and social construct that varies depending on the culture (Association of College and Research Libraries, 2015). The ACRL frame, "Scholarship as Conversation" is also discussed to show students the importance of recognizing and appreciating the larger, ongoing body of research on a particular topic (Schvaneveldt et al., 2021). For example, librarians utilize the *National Dental Association Journal* and the *Journal of the National Medical Association* as resources to address health equity in oral health and medical care disparities. Students are given topics and encouraged to search for articles in these two journals for classroom engagement and discussion.

Key Strategies for the Future of Cultural Humility in Dental Curricula

Based on our perspectives in the field, three key strategies have emerged to effectively integrate cultural humility among predoctoral dental training curricula (see Table 7.1). Overall, these strategies focus on the inclusion of cultural humility among didactic and clinical experiences, usage of librarian resources to promote cultural humility as an applicable clinical skill, and the assessment of how cultural humility has been integrated into the predoctoral dental curricula. They provide insight for dental programs to take a closer look at how their cultural climate, infrastructure, and processes can better support cultural humility within their dental curricula.

CONCLUSION

As dental education evolves continuously to reflect the biomedical and behavioral needs of diverse populations, the need to deliver culturally responsive care is inevitable. While the perspectives in this chapter yield a descriptive insight on how cultural humility is and can be operationalized within dental curricula, further collective action is necessary for sustainability. Furthermore, the partnership of librarians with their dental programs can cultivate a novel opportunity to create capacity and space within the curricula for cultural humility learning objectives. Curricula with learning objectives that are applied

Table 7.1. Cultural Humility Strategies for Predoctoral Dental Training Curricula

Cultural Humility Strategy	Description
Librarian-Specific Resources for Cultural Humility	Librarians should continue to add cultural humility resources to their local dental school collections. Furthermore, a robust promotion of resources should occur through library guides and instruction, student workshops, and faculty meetings. This will elevate additional opportunities for librarians, faculty, and students to genuinely work to develop real appreciation of cultural differences and reciprocal respect.
Advancing Cultural Humility through Didactic and Clinical Experiences	Faculty and librarians should collaborate to create capacity and room within the predoctoral dental curricula to teach cultural humility. To facilitate this capacity, a rigorous crosswalk within the predoctoral dental curricula should occur to examine current courses with the capacity to align cultural humility learning objectives, feasible course deliverables, and course type (i.e., didactic and/or clinical course). To address any gaps, consider developing new courses with the incorporation of librarians as an integral facet.
Assess the Impact of Cultural Humility among the Predoctoral Dental Curricula	Institution-specific competencies and practices associated with student efficacy for cultural humility should be assessed. Integral and/or annual cohort survey assessments can support a specific understanding of how learning objectives for both didactic and clinical courses integrate cultural humility as part of the predoctoral dental curricula.

in didactic and clinical settings support the preparation of a dental workforce that practices cultural humility for the delivery of quality dental care.

ACKNOWLEDGMENT

Irene Lubker would like to acknowledge Amanda Nevius, former librarian at Tufts University, for kindly allowing usage and adaption of her content for anti-racism in dentistry and for coteaching the anti-racism workshop on November 16, 2021, at the Medical University of South Carolina, James B. Edwards College of Dental Medicine, Charleston.

REFERENCES

Alrqiq, H. M., Scott, T. E., & Mascarenhas, A. K. (2015). Evaluating a cultural competency curriculum: Changes in dental students' perceived awareness, knowledge, and skills. *Journal of Dental Education, 79*(9), 1009–1015. https://79/9/1009 [pii]

American Dental Education Association. (2020). *ADEA access, diversity and inclusion framework 1-1*. https://www.adea.org/diversity/framework/

Association of College and Research Libraries. (2015). *Framework for information literacyfor higher education*. https://www.ala.org/acrl/standards/ilframework

Coelho, K. R., & Galan, C. (2012). Physician cross-cultural nonverbal communication skills, patient satisfaction and health outcomes in the physician-patient relationship. *International Journal of Family Medicine, 2012,* 376907. https://10.1155/2012/376907

Commission on Dental Accreditation. (2020) *Accreditation for dental education programs*. https://coda.ada.org/

Cook, B. J. (2016). *Moving from anecdote to analytics*. [PowerPoint slides]. Educational Research and Analysis Department. American Dental Education Association.

Daugherty, H. N., & Kearney, R. C. (2017). Measuring the impact of cultural competence training for dental hygiene students. *Journal of Dental Hygiene, 91*(5), 48–54.

Goodman, X. Y., & Nugent, R. L. (2020). Teaching cultural competence and cultural humility in dental medicine. *Medical Reference Services Quarterly, 39*(4), 309–322. https://10.1080/02763869.2020.1826183

Hodge, T. (2019). Integrating cultural humility into public services librarianship. *International Information & Library Review, 51*(3), 268–274. https://10.1080/10572317.2019.1629070

MUSC James B. College of Dental Medicine Dental Faculty Meeting. (2020). *MUSC James B. College of Dental Medicine, 2025 strategy*.

MUSC Office of Diversity and Inclusion. (2020) *Medical University of South Carolina strategic plan for diversity & inclusion*. https://web.musc.edu/-/sm/enterprise/about/leadership/institutional-offices/diversity/f/di-strategic-plan.ashx

Office of Diversity for the MUSC James B. Edwards College of Dental Medicine. (2022). *Office of Diversity for the College of Dental Medicine*. Office of Diversity of the College of Dental Medicine. https://dentistry.musc.edu/programs/diversity

Pilcher, E. S., Charles, L. T., & Lancaster, C. J. (2008). Development and assessment of a cultural competency curriculum. *Journal of Dental Education, 72*(9), 1020–1028. https://72/9/1020 [pii]

Schvaneveldt, N., Stone, S. M., Brody, E. R., Clairoux, N., Lubker, I. M., Nevius, A. M., Porcello, L., & Bissram, J. S. (2021). Aligning information literacy and evidence-based dentistry concepts in a rubric to improve dental education.

Medical Reference Services Quarterly, 40(2), 236–248. https://10.1080/02763869.2021.1912580

Solchanyk, D., Ekeh, O., Saffran, L., Burnett-Zeigler, I. E., & Doobay-Persaud, A. (2021). Integrating cultural humility into the medical education curriculum: Strategies for educators. *Teaching and Learning in Medicine, 33*(5), 554–560. https://doi.org/10.1080/10401334.2021.1877711

Sushner, N. I. (1977). A photographic study of the soft-tissue profile of the Negro population. *American Journal of Orthodontics, 72*(4), 373–385. https://10.1016/0002-9416(77)90350-5

Tervalon, M., & Murray-Garcia, J. (1998). Cultural humility versus cultural competence: a critical distinction in defining physician training outcomes in multicultural education. *Journal of Health Care for the Poor and Underserved, 9*(2), 117–125. https://10.1353/hpu.2010.0233

Thom, D. H., Tirado, M. D., Woon, T. L., & McBride, M. R. (2006). Development and evaluation of a cultural competency training curriculum. *BMC Medical Education, 6,* (38). https://1472-6920-6-38 [pii]

Trinh NH, Jahan AB, Chen JA. Moving from Cultural Competence to Cultural Humility in Psychiatric Education. Psychiatr Clin North Am. 2021 Jun; 44(2):149–157. doi: 10.1016/j.psc.2020.12.002. Epub 2021 Apr 29. PMID:34049639.

U.S. Department of Health and Human Resources—Office of Minority Health. (2013). *National standards for culturally and linguistically appropriate services (CLAS) in health and health care.* https://thinkculturalhealth.hhs.gov/clas

Venditto, V. J., & Colón, K. (2022). Promoting cultural humility by integrating health equity literature into the pharmacy curriculum. *Pharmacy (Basel, Switzerland), 10*(5), 116. doi: 10.3390/pharmacy10050116. https://10.3390/pharmacy10050116

8

Building Connections, Crucial Conversations, and Cross-Cultural Relationships

Xan Y. Goodman and Twanna Hodge

Throughout the changing landscapes of life, there are lessons to be learned and opportunities for further growth and deepened relationships. In this chapter, we will explore cultural humility (CH) in the context of building connections within cross-cultural relationships and crucial conversations (CC). We will define and explain how to build connections and cross-cultural relationships and how crucial conversations contribute to creating relationships that are grounded in humility. In our conclusion, we will share lessons learned, practical strategies, and challenges faced.

BUILDING CONNECTIONS

To build and reframe connections, crucial conversations, and cross-cultural relationships, you must start with yourself. To begin cultivating awareness about your own cultural background, start with examining cultural humility–related characteristics. These characteristics may help to identify pathways to openness as you may not know everything about your culture. We have identified the following characteristics of CH developed by Zhu et al. (2021, 7).

1. Openness to cultural multiplicity
2. Lifelong self-examination

3. Interpersonal modesty
4. Lack of defensiveness
5. Relational orientation
6. Allowing growth through the professional life span

We believe that the characteristics outlined by Zhu et al. (2021) are a good first step toward building connections, while keeping in mind that it will take consistent time, effort, and reflection.

An openness to cultural multiplicity and cultural curiosity that is self-oriented and other-oriented is necessary. This centers on embracing openness about one's cultural multiplicities, curiosity about one's own culture, and an outward orientation toward openness about others. To build on this are the three pillars of CH: (1) commit to learning, (2) act to remove power imbalances, and (3) commit to connection (Goodman, 2019). Figure 8.1 provides a visual description of CH and contextualizes it as a concept influenced by the social context while also being grounded in historical and political precedence.

Lifelong self-examination includes having a growth mindset and enacting lifelong learning as a core practice. Additionally, interpersonal modesty, intellectual humility, and lack of defensiveness are essential to a life we want to have. Whereas relational orientation emphasizes how one is in a relationship

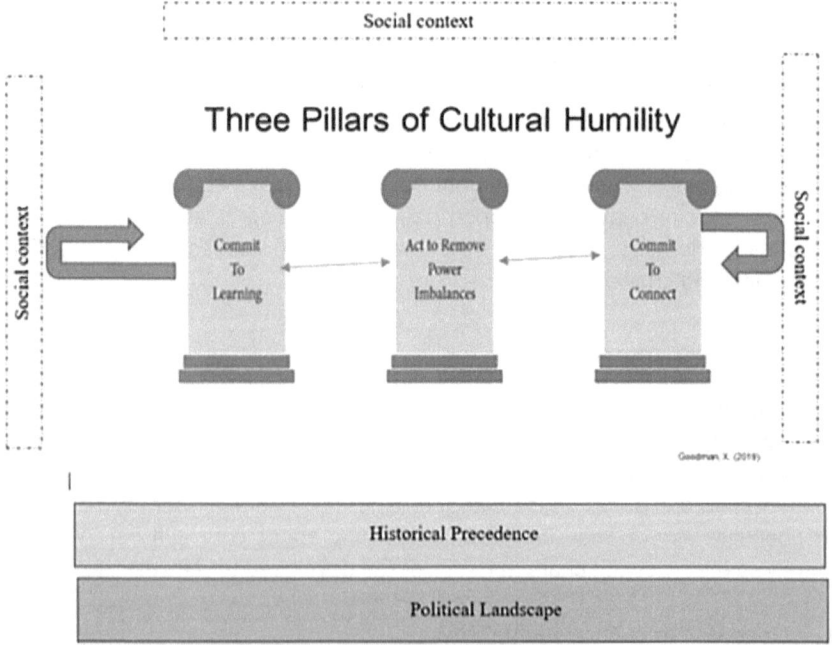

Figure 8.1. Three Pillars of Cultural Humility.

with others. We suggest that actively monitoring these characteristics in oneself and being actively intentional is key to cultivating connection.

Connections with Colleagues and Patrons

Listening to the stories of our colleagues and patrons allows us to create connections (Brown, 2021). Yet creating connections with others requires effort. Effort involves the ability to engage in labor and have the psychological capacity to listen, in addition to possessing emotional intelligence. Vulnerability and risk-taking are aspects of emotional intelligence (Brown, 2021; Goleman, 2020).

Telling one's story requires effort and the ability to listen deeply and with humility. Shame, humiliation, and guilt are barriers to initiating connection. Shame might stop us from sharing our stories (Burke & Brown, 2021). A connection is something that one cannot rush or force others to take on. Consider the following in your efforts to build or create that connection:

- What are the possible impacts? What resources will it take?
- How long can you invest in building the connection?
- How will you sustain it?
- How would you conclude a connection?
- What are some additional barriers people face when building connections?
- What were some of the challenges faced during the pandemic that either fostered connections or exacerbated disconnection and isolation?

We also recommend being able to read the room and discern when to build a connection. Having the ability to read social and emotional cues will also aid in building connections, while considering the needs of people with differing abilities and those who are neurodiverse. Though it may be challenging, communicating clearly, respectfully, and empathetically is necessary to help cultivate bonds while respecting boundaries.

Schein and Schein (2018) describe different levels of relationships in their book *Humble Leadership*. They refer to four levels of relationships, with the most effective being a Level 2. Level 2 relationships are not built on transactions but instead upon respect and genuine interest. The connection then becomes an opportunity to extend and expand the way we operate within our work environments, while keeping in mind that deep connections are not formed with every colleague or patron. Library work is frequently a sum of transactions, gate counts, number of computers used, instruction sessions held, and various metrics associated with these activities, technologies, or individuals. These measurements form the calculus that we utilize to assess who uses our services, making library work inherently transactional in nature. The degree of transactional focus within the structure of libraries may seep into the relationships with patrons and colleagues.

Authenticity in building connections is a factor in reframing transactional relationships in libraries. In her TEDx talk on authenticity, Jodi-Ann Burey (2020) explains that, as a Black woman, she chooses not to bring her whole self to work. Burey has set a comfortable boundary that agrees with her positionality. As library workers seeking to build connections with patrons and coworkers, we need to keep in mind that colleagues and patrons vary in how much of their authentic, whole selves they bring into the library environment. We recommend pondering these three points to build connections: (1) listening—actively and willingly—as a humble practice to share beyond transactions, (2) setting boundaries that keep you whole and safe, and (3) choosing your level of authenticity at work. Barksdale-Hall (2022) reminds library workers to connect to their core values by writing personal reflections and pursuing personal healing. While Roquemore and Laszloffy (2008) suggests that tenure-track academics consider getting a therapist to endure the more than likely vicissitudes of academia, we suggest this recommendation for any library worker in academia. Later in the chapter, we will discuss how personal background, including trauma, might hinder connections in cross-cultural relationships.

Connections with Communities

Though people make up workplaces, the culture of an organization may not lend itself to centering humanness or considering the humanness of creating connection. Building connection extends beyond the relationships of library workers and patrons in physical libraries. Cultural humility also requires connecting to communities to create success together. This part of CH is fraught with questions as library workers battle and might succumb to vocational awe, deauthentication, mission creep, and low morale (Ettarh, 2018; Kendrick, 2017; Kendrick & Damasco, 2019; Kendrick, 2020). "Vocational awe describes the set of ideas, values, and assumptions librarians have about themselves and the profession that result in notions that libraries as institutions are inherently good, sacred notions, and therefore beyond critique" (Ettarh, 2018). Ettarh's description of vocational awe is a cautionary signal for library workers who might succumb to the view of libraries as pristine locations of work devoid of social context. This stance might construct unnecessary barriers to building strong connections. Certainly, vocational awe might lack the CH characteristics mentioned by Zhu et al. (2021), creating further distance from humble practices.

"Deauthentication is a cognitive process to prepare for or navigate predominantly White workplace environments. This process results in decisions that hide or reduce aspects of the influence of ethnic, racial, or cultural identities, etc. Furthermore, deauthentication decisions are made to avoid macro- or microaggressions, shaming, incivility, punishment, or retaliation, and these decisions ultimately create barriers to sharing whole selves with colleagues and/or clients" (Kendrick & Damasco, 2019). Professionalism, workplace codes of conduct, unspoken or unwritten rules of civility or collegiality, and the prevailing organizational culture contribute to the level of deauthentication that people experience both within and beyond the organization.

In this case, CH is built on the political landscape and historical precedence of community relations. In her chapter "Libraries and the Color Line," Evans (2022) describes how library histories gloss over the complicity of libraries that upheld the American apartheid system of barriers to access. These barriers were present in all types of libraries for both patrons and library workers. In *Pushing the Margins*, Freeman (2017) describes the erasure of Black women from histories, including librarianship. These examples encourage us to interrogate both political and historical precedence as the foundation on which CH stands. Ask such questions about political and historical precedence to apply to community connections as:

- What is the historical context of the library?
- What about the political context?
- How did these come to exist?

These are only a few questions to begin a thoughtful inquiry, as we often forget that libraries are institutions situated in communities. Contemplate what has happened with community connections in the past. and the library's relationship to that, including any outreach that staff have done in the community. When reestablishing community connections or forming new ones, you might ask:

- Why is the outreach effort being undertaken?
- What resources will it require?
- How long can you invest in building the connection?
- How will you build succession planning to sustain a connection?
- What are some of the barriers people face when building connections?

In light of the profound changes experienced globally by communities during the COVID-19 pandemic, you could ask how this affected building connections. We anticipate that the ramifications of the pandemic may have created ongoing challenges for libraries.

These are practical realities to consider when building connections in the workplace. In the following section, we discuss how crucial conversations are a practical next step to building connections. As libraries seek to practice CH and connect to communities, deliberate attention to how the library's organizational culture supports these connections is vital. Valuing community relationships by creating infrastructure to foster depth and longevity to the community is an element of CH.

CRUCIAL CONVERSATIONS

Crucial conversations are essential to ground your connection in cultural humility. Grenny et al., (2022) describe a crucial conversation as "a discussion between two or more people in which they hold opposing opinions about a high stakes issue and where emotions run strong" (Grenny et al., 2022, 3). We describe practical crucial conversations as those that help build connections by establishing healthy boundaries for more meaningful connections. To have a crucial conversation in the context of establishing a relationship will also include (1) acknowledging mistakes, (2) being aware of your positionality, (3) being attentive to power dynamics and redressing power imbalances, and (4) acknowledging emotions with body awareness.

Mistakes occur in the course of relationships in our interactions with colleagues or patrons. An important thing to remember is to acknowledge a mistake. One way we see this in libraries is in the changing conversation and approach about patron fines. While not explicitly saying libraries have made a mistake, library policymakers are recognizing the importance of shifting away from fines and changing this practical crucial conversation point with patrons. Likewise, admitting our mistakes and faux pas in relationships with colleagues is a CH practice. To read more about crucial conversations and emotional intelligence, we recommend Grenny et al. (2022), *Crucial Conversations: Tools for Talking When the Stakes Are High*, and *Emotional Intelligence: Why It Can Matter More than IQ* by Daniel Goleman (2015).

We use the term "positionality" here to describe how power might be enacted from a position. Being aware of positionality leads to a broader understanding of power dynamics and a willingness to redress power imbalances. Positionality might include power one may have in relation to patrons (Coghlan & Brydon-Miller, 2014). Library workers, especially supervisors, might also have power over staff who are under their purview. We assert that CH does require acknowledging positionality and redressing power imbalances.

Consequently, we want to emphasize that crucial conversations involve emotions, so we offer a few questions for reflection: How do you know when you are ready to have a crucial conversation? Do you have the psychological space to have the conversation? Keeping a close watch on your emotional intelligence and self-awareness about your given state might dictate your ability to manage a crucial conversation. Realizing that you may not know the limits, capacities, and triggers of those whom you are connecting with, while also accepting others' boundaries, "nos," and vulnerabilities can present a challenge.

Being aware of others' emotional reactions, as well as how your own emotions may show up during a crucial conversation, is vital to the response. This requires a certain amount of mindfulness about your own ways of managing emotion and how you handle vulnerability with others. One way to handle this is to validate what you feel with mindfulness and self-checking, while also validating what your conversation partner is expressing, by asking yourself:

- How am I doing, honestly?
- What is happening with my emotions?
- How is my body experiencing this conversation?
- How am I communicating my emotions?

After all, libraries are full of people who connect daily with one another. Patrons connect with library workers, library workers connect with one another, and stakeholders provide support to libraries who connect. These are all relationships that require boundaries. When it is time to communicate, consider using assertive communication (Kendrick, 2020). In March 2020, as the world began to shut down, many of us found our inboxes filled with invitations for virtual meetups with colleagues, ranging from happy hours to crafting events to teatimes. At the same time, many may have found themselves stretching work into the evenings and weekends. For some, the virtual environment allowed for Zoom intimacy, while for others, it presented an invasion of privacy and a heightened level of surveillance. As we sheltered in place, we brought all our work worlds into our personal worlds, creating discomfort, challenging transactions, and other obstacles for many of us. Some of us constructed workspaces in our homes, which may have ended up encroaching on our personal lives. When we began writing this chapter in 2022, the global pandemic was still going on, and some of the conditions from 2020 still linger. The pandemic created a unique opportunity to build connections and hold crucial conversations as well.

Employee resource groups (ERGs) are based on a demographic characteristic, life phase, or other aspect of identity. These groups have been around for over fifty years, with the first being established in Rochester, New York, by employees at Xerox (Welbourne et al., 2015). There is some usefulness in being able to join an ERG as it could provide an outlet to expressing oneself or serve as an informal channel for organizational information. On a diverse and densely populated campus, ERGs may be more plentiful. However, finding an ERG could be challenging in a situation where a person is the sole BIPOC individual in a library work setting, which is not uncommon in some libraries. Because most ERGs are run by volunteers, this presents an extra service burden for marginalized personnel who usually volunteer to staff these groups.

In our experience, informal networks that are not associated with formal ERGs provide more support. During the pandemic, the African American Medical Librarians Alliance Caucus (AAMLA) formed a Chat & Chew group that was affinity based but not employee based. AAMLA connected Black library workers focused on health sciences or medical librarianship from around the

United States. Other groups, such as the American Library Association (ALA) Spectrum Scholars, and the Black Caucus of the ALA (BCALA), have proved more supportive than formal ERGs. If a group of this nature exists at your workplace, we suggest visiting with the group to determine if it will meet your needs for connection.

To build connections and hold crucial conversations we must maintain an awareness about our capacity to have CC, while also giving grace to those with whom we engage. Grenny et al., (2022) suggest that you:

- Consider the factual and narrative elements behind the catalyst for the conversation.
- Evaluate the emotions you are holding and expressing.
- Reflect on some patterns you might typically cycle into.
- Be assertive yet compassionate while expressing your views and hearing others express their point of view (if possible, establish norms to rebuild safety).
- Work toward mutual purpose and encourage mutual respect.
- Apologize when appropriate.
- Address any past or current misunderstandings.

Identify and focus on what you really want, ask for their perspective, and mirror what you are observing through questions like, "I am observing X, is this correct?" Paraphrase what was communicated to you, ask priming questions such as, "Do you think that ... ?" and then determine what needs to happen next if a follow-up is necessary. The humble practice of active listening, including asking good questions, fits well here. Listening well includes using paraphrasing skills or mirroring, along with asking good open-ended follow-up questions (Brown, 2021).

Remember, your previous personal and professional history will impact your approach and CC process. Be conscious that conflict avoidance may harm and lead to heightened negative emotions. Passive aggressiveness, "library nice" (major dependence and adherence to politeness and niceties), and respectability politics can block CC from starting or being concluded in a way that benefits those who are participants. The right to comfort is a characteristic embedded in librarianship influenced by white supremacy culture. Centering white comfort instead of addressing issues when they arise leads to unhealthy and toxic relationships and environments (DiAngelo, 2021; Okun, n.d.). Avoiding crucial conversations can lead to personnel issues and may involve salary negotiations, scheduling coordination, microaggressions, or biased incidents. Remember that CC could involve any situation with opposing viewpoints, high stakes, and heightened emotions. Our relationships and work environments depend on having CC and becoming comfortable with being uncomfortable. Maintaining healthy connections, relationships, and communities depends on it. Our differences are benefits and assets that can help our profession, communities, and relationships become more diverse and cross-cultural.

CROSS-CULTURAL RELATIONSHIPS AND BUILDING CONNECTIONS

Relationships are complex and nuanced. Cross-cultural relationships are between persons who come from different cultural backgrounds (Johnson & Cullen, 2017). Where you were born and/or raised has impacted and molded your understanding of the world and how you create and maintain relationships. There is a need to have empathy and allow for growth in relationships. For Black, Indigenous, and People of Color (BIPOC), the pressure to adhere to professionalism norms based on whiteness is a major burden in the workplace, as their identities may not align with allowing vulnerability, given the expected standards and organizational culture. People in the BIPOC community are constantly under pressure to put themselves in boxes, centering our professional identity and engaging in deauthentication. Communicating across differences to develop and maintain healthy relationships is critical to the work we are doing (Hurn & Tomalin 2013), Cross-cultural communication involves the interactions and exchanges of people from different cultures when they communicate at a distance or face-to-face. Communication can involve spoken and written language, as well as nonverbal aspects like body language, etiquette, and protocol.

A core tenet of CH is being other-oriented. As you engage in a conversation, consider what you know and do not know about your culture and the culture of the other person. Neither of your cultures can be distilled to a list of attributes or characteristics, and what you observe is only one layer of the complexity of the person you are communicating with. "Intercultural communication is a symbolic process in which people from different cultures create shared meanings" (Hurn & Tomalin, 2013, p. 44). Within Black librarianship, there is a greater diversity that needs to be acknowledged. In the chapter "Assumed Identities: Realities of Afro-Caribbean Librarians," the coauthors, despite having different Caribbean heritage, find that their distinct identities are often erased due to the concept of Blackness in the United States (Hodge et al., 2022). Consequently, the authors had to learn how to navigate American culture and create relationships with different Americans. Even when we seem to be the same, there are deeper differences and identities to be understood and supported.

We all have hopes, wishes, dreams, desires, and more, and we want to be acknowledged, feel celebrated, and know that we truly belong. We need to continue to create and support spaces where we allow each other to grow—over the professional life span and throughout the journey, as we all remain works in progress. Cultural humility urges us to push back against our own biases by challenging ourselves to learn more about those we engage with. The challenge lies in not dismissing or tokenizing people based on their identities but rather acknowledging their identities and considering all aspects of who they are. For example, the Black community experiences colorism based on skin tone.

Even in professional relationships and contexts, the histories of our personal lives form the fertile ground that emerges in our relationships. Library workers and patrons are not spared of their upbringing as they enter libraries. How someone was raised and their exposures to toxicity and negativity impact their ability to form connections (hooks, 2015). In *The Body Keeps the Score: Brain, Mind, and Body in the Healing of Trauma*, Van der Kolk (2014) describes the impact of adverse childhood experiences (ACEs) on developing relationships. Extending Van der Kolk's (2014) work to librarianship, we can anticipate that there are folks in libraries who have experienced some form of trauma. To account for these aspects of trauma, there is new focus on trauma librarianship that acknowledges personal traumas and the ascending recognition of intergenerational trauma. In Tolley's book *A Trauma-Informed Approach to Library Services*, "trauma-informed approach (TIA) acknowledges that there are many contributing factors (known and unknown, micro to macro, historical to current, visible and invisible) that affect individuals, how they navigate and interact in the world, and how they engage in the services provided" (Hodge, 2021, 780).

LESSONS LEARNED, PRACTICAL STRATEGIES, AND CHALLENGES FACED

Here are some lessons learned, practical strategies, and challenges faced that incorporate content from building connections, crucial conversations, and cross-cultural relationships. This is not a comprehensive list, but we encourage you to engage in self-reflection to connect with your core values and practice mindful awareness of how your body feels in any situation, especially when engaging in a crucial conversation.

Lessons Learned

- Be kind to yourself.
- Be kind to others.
- Acknowledge that everyone is in a different place on their journey just as you are. This requires meeting people where they are.
- Do not try to avoid mistakes and conflict; it will happen.
- Learn to be comfortable through discomfort.
- Practice patience and grace.
- Make time for relationship building with individuals and communities; it takes time.
- Know when to walk away.
- Acknowledge when you are self-sabotaging.

- Know when a person, group, or communication is no longer good for you.
- Acknowledge when a professional relationship is negative, unhealthy, or toxic.
- Engage in counseling or therapy to address ACEs, as well as recent and current traumas.
- Define your own authenticity.

Practical Strategies

- Open-mindedness
- Mindfulness; being aware of your breath, emotions, and thoughts
- Acknowledging mistakes
- Being aware of your positionality
- Being aware of the power you hold
- Power dynamics and redressing power imbalances
- Identity and identity development
- Self-reflection
- Accountability
- Training
- Community of practice/support network
- Ongoing education/lifelong learning

Challenges You May Face

- Vocational awe
- White supremacy culture characteristics
- Time
- (White) savior complex
- Internalized oppression
- Insecurities
- Mission creep

Questions to Ask Yourself

- What are some current practical strategies that can be developed for building and maintaining connections?
- What are some challenges and rewards related to building connections?
- How can I be successful and help others achieve success?

CONCLUSION

In this chapter, we explored cultural humility (CH) in the context of building connections within cross-cultural relationships and crucial conversations (CC). We defined and explained practical strategies for and challenges to building connections and cross-cultural relationships and holding crucial conversations that are grounded in humility. We emphasized using humble practices and cultural humility characteristics (Zhu et al., 2021) as ways to enact cultural humility as a library worker.

The lessons learned, practical strategies discussed, and challenges faced may be familiar or new, but they present opportunities to interrogate our understanding of relationships and to continue growing in centering the humanity of ourselves and others in building connections and engaging in crucial conversations. We have an unprecedented opportunity to create and try new strategies for building connections and establishing a new normal, post-pandemic and beyond. We encourage you to reflect on the words of beloved scholar, writer, artist, and teacher bell hooks: "we need to center love, love of community, love of ourselves, of others and the communities that we serve" (hooks, 2001).

REFERENCES

Barksdale-Hall, R. (2022). Uhuru celebration of individual and collective healing and empowerment: Five lessons from an activist librarian-author-griot. In S. Burns-Simpson, M. M. Hayes, A. Ndumu, & S. Walker (eds.), *The Black librarian in America: Reflections, resistance, and reawakening* (pp. 123–140). Rowman & Littlefield.

Brown, B. (2021). *Atlas of the heart: Mapping meaningful connection and the language of the human experience.* Random House.

Burey, J. A. (2020, November). *The myth of bringing your full, authentic self to work* [Video file]. TEDx Seattle. https://www.ted.com/talks/jodi_ann_burey_the_myth_of_bringing_your_full_authentic_self_to_work

Burke, T., & Brown, B. (2021). *You are the best thing: Vulnerability, shame, resilience, and the black experience.* Random House.

Coghlan, D. & Brydon-Miller, M. (2014). Positionality. In D. Coghlan (ed.), *SAGE encyclopedia of action research.* (p. 628). Sage Publications.

DiAngelo, R. (2021). *Nice white racism: How progressive white people perpetuate harm.* Beacon Press.

Ettarh, F. (2018, January 10). *Vocational awe and librarianship: The lies we tell ourselves.* In the Library with the Lead Pipe. https://www.inthelibrarywiththeleadpipe.org/2018/vocational-awe/

Evans, R. (2022). Libraries and the color line: DuBois and the matter of representation. In S. Burns-Simpson, M. M. Hayes, A. Ndumu, & S. Walker (eds.), *The Black librarian in America: Reflections, resistance, and reawakening* (pp. 9–24). Rowman & Littlefield.

Freeman, J. E. (2017). When will my reflection show? Women of color in the Kennesaw State University Archives. In R. L. Chou & A. Pho (eds.), *Pushing the margins: Women of color and intersectionality in LIS* (pp. 391–414). Library Juice Press.

Goleman, D. (2020). *Emotional intelligence, Why It Can Matter More Than IQ* (Twenty-fifth anniversary). Bloomsbury Publishing.

Goodman, X. (2019). *Cultural humility in action.* https://library.ca.gov/wp-content/uploads/2021/08/Cultural_Humility_in_Public_Libraries.pdf

Grenny. J., Patterson, K., McMillian, R., Switzler, A., Gregory, E. (2022). *Crucial conversations: Tools for talking when stakes are high.* 3rd edition. McGraw Hill.

Hodge, T. (2021). Book reviews. [Review of the book *A trauma-informed approach to library services*, by Rebecca Tolley]. *College & Research Libraries,* 82(5), 780. https://crl.acrl.org/index.php/crl/article/view/25025/32903

Hodge, T., Bartley, K., & Flash, K. (2022). Assumed identities: Realities of Afro-Caribbean librarians. In S. Burns-Simpson, M. M. Hayes, A. Ndumu, & S. Walker (eds.), *The Black librarian in America: Reflections, resistance, and reawakening* (pp. 73–89). Rowman & Littlefield.

hooks, b. (2001). *All about love: New visions.* William Morrow.

hooks, b. (2015). *Sisters of the yam: Black women and self-recovery.* Routledge.

Hurn B. J., & Tomalin B. (2013). What is cross-cultural communication? In M. W. Lustig & J. Koester (eds.), *Cross-Cultural Communication* (p. 44). Palgrave Macmillan. https://doi.org/10.1057/9780230391147_1

Johnson, J. L., & Cullen, J. B. (2017). Trust in cross-cultural relationships. In M. J. Gannon & K. L. Newman (eds.), *The Blackwell handbook of cross-cultural management* (chap. 17). Blackwell Publishers Ltd. https://doi.org/10.1002/9781405164030.ch17

Kendrick, K. D. (2017). The low morale experience of academic librarians: A phenomenological study. *Journal of Library Administration, 57*(8), 846–878. https://doi.org/10.1080/01930826.2017.1368325

Kendrick, K. D. (2020). The public librarian low-morale experience: A qualitative study. *Partnership: The Canadian Journal of Library & Information Practice & Research, 15*(2), 1–32. https://doi.org/10.21083/partnership.v15i2.5932

Kendrick, K. D., & Damasco, I. T. (2019). Low morale in ethnic and racial minority academic librarians: An experiential study. *Library Trends, 68*(2), 174–212. https://doi.org/10.1353/lib.2019.0036

Okun, T. (n.d.) *White supremacy culture: Dismantling racism.* http://www.dismantlingracism.org/uploads/4/3/5/7/43579015/whitesupcul13.pdf

Roquemore, K. A., & Laszloffy, T. (2008). *The Black academic's guide to winning tenure without losing our soul.* Lynne Rienner Publishers.

Schein, E. H., & Schein, P. A. (2018). *Humble leadership: The power of relationships, openness, and trust.* 1st ed. Berrett-Koehler Publishers.

Van der Kolk, B. (2014). *The body keeps the score: Brain, mind, and body in the healing of trauma.* Viking.

Welbourne, T. M., Rolf, S., & Schlachter, S. (2015). Employee resource groups: An introduction, review and research agenda. *Academy of Management*

Proceedings, 2015(1), 15661. https://ceo.usc.edu/wp-content/uploads/2015/05/2015-13-G15-13-660-ERG_Introduction_Review_Research.pdf

Zhu, P., Liu, Y., Luke, M. M., Wang, Q. (2021) The development and initial validation of the cultural humility and enactment scale in counseling. *Measurement and Evaluation in Counseling and Development*, https://doi.org/10.1080/07481756.2021.1955215

9

Securing Your Mask First

INTEGRATING CULTURAL HUMILITY INTO YOUR LEADERSHIP PRACTICE

Shannon D. Jones and Beverly Murphy

Whenever you fly on an airplane, the flight attendant instructs you to "put your oxygen mask on first" before helping others. This is an important rule for ensuring survival, because if you run out of oxygen yourself, you can't help anyone else with their oxygen mask. *Putting your oxygen mask on first* means taking care of yourself. Taking care of yourself requires self-reflection and self-critique. Both concepts allow you to interrogate your assumptions, perspectives, beliefs, values, and daily actions and examine their impact on your professional and personal relationships.

Self-reflection and self-critique are the root of cultural humility. Tervalon and Murray-Garcia (1998) define cultural humility "as a lifelong commitment to self-evaluation and critique, to redressing the power imbalances ... and to developing mutually beneficial and non-paternalistic partnerships with communities on behalf of individuals and defined populations" (p. 123). Hook et al. (2013) add, cultural humility is the "ability to maintain an interpersonal stance that is other-oriented (or open to the other) in relation to aspects of cultural identity that are most important to the [person]" (p. 2). In the grand scheme of our leadership actions, everything we do is about people. How we lead them is important, but equally important are the methods we use to value, center, and appreciate the unique perspectives and otherness that people bring to our spaces. The journey toward becoming a culturally humble practitioner is about the actions we take toward caring and appreciating others by first taking care of ourselves.

Leaders who operate with humility work to ensure that people around them feel safe, valued, heard, seen, appreciated, and included. Cultivating an environment where the individuals around you feel like they matter is the result of intentionality. This chapter explores the meaning of cultural humility in leadership and unpacks what it looks like in everyday practice. This exploration must first begin by defining what it is not. Words like "arrogant," "narcissistic," "self-serving," and "self-centered" come to mind when thinking of leaders who do not practice humility. The purpose of this chapter is to describe what cultural humility looks like when an individual enacts best practice concepts in their approach to leading. The authors share lessons learned from activating and experiencing humility in their leadership approaches.

WHY PRACTICING CULTURAL HUMILITY IS IMPORTANT

Dominance of the "Isms"

The primary reason that all of us should work to integrate cultural humility into our daily practice is due to the pervasive presence of the "isms" (such as racism, sexism, classism, ableism, anti-Semitism, ageism, sizeism, and heterosexism). We are living in a world in 2023 where prejudice and discrimination resulting from the "isms" are at the forefront. Long gone are the days when it was politically incorrect or socially unacceptable to publicly use racial slurs or mock people with disabilities. Hate speech used to be relegated to private, off-the-record conversations, not the nightly news or social media.

This all changed in 2007 when Barack Obama announced his candidacy for the forty-fourth president of the United States (POTUS), and it exacerbated the problem further with his election in 2008. The level of disrespect aimed at President Obama throughout his eight years in office was blatant. But just when it seemed as if things could not get any worse, Donald Trump was elected as the forty-fifth POTUS in 2016. Throughout his presidency, Trump amplified hate speech while normalizing disrespect and the "isms." Tension in local communities was palpable, and civility seemed to be a thing of the past. Following the conclusion of Donald Trump's presidency, we're compelled to reflect on the detrimental impact of "isms" against marginalized groups, encompassing misunderstandings, discontent, mistrust, lost opportunities, and deferred dreams. This has led to long-term and, in some cases, irrevocable psychological, physiological, and emotional trauma.

Diversity Is Increasing

Practicing cultural humility is also important because the world is becoming more diverse than ever. The business case for integrating cultural humility into one's daily practice is twofold.

1. *The U.S. population is becoming more diverse.* Statistics from the U.S. Census projects that "the nation will become 'minority white' in 2045 when whites will comprise 49.7 percent of the population in contrast to 24.6 percent for Hispanics, 13.1 percent for blacks, 7.9 percent for Asians, and 3.8 percent for multiracial populations" (Frey, 2018). With more diversity in the world, differences will be amplified, making it necessary that all of us are able to communicate across cultures and the dimensions of diversity.
2. *Diversity is a competitive advantage.* Phillips (2014) says,
   Diversity enhances creativity. It encourages the search for novel information and perspectives, leading to better decision-making and problem-solving. Diversity can improve the bottom line of companies and lead to unfettered discoveries and breakthrough innovations. Even simply being exposed to diversity can change the way you think. This is not just wishful thinking: it is the conclusion we draw from decades of research from organizational scientists, psychologists, sociologists, economists, and demographers (para 3).

Library workers must be prepared to engage with and support colleagues while providing services to patrons whose lived experiences are different from their own. Adopting a practice undergirded by compassion, empathy, kindness, authenticity, respect, and understanding is required for working in twenty-first-century libraries. This is especially true for those of us who serve as library leaders. Leaders who practice humility should strive to cultivate environments where all individuals feel safe, welcome, seen, heard, valued, and included. We should honor, acknowledge, and celebrate the unique differences and perspectives that people bring to the environment. Most importantly, our spaces should emit a sense of belonging as a priority, allowing individuals to make real connections with one another. Cultural humility is the key to building meaningful connections.

Building better connections with individuals whose lived experiences differ from our own has the potential to enrich our lives. The same is true in our workplaces. Assembling a diverse group of individuals to solve challenges and develop solutions is beneficial to our libraries and the clientele we serve. Boesen (2012) shares, "Connecting with others requires patience, kindness and understanding. At times, our connection with others may be blocked by our personal "culture" that does not allow us to recognize and appreciate the differences in others" (para 1). Rigger (2018) adds, "An investment in diversity is an investment in top talent, new ideas and better connections" (para 1). Creating environments where cultural humility can thrive will be the result of leaders that are culturally humble. In the next section, we describe the actions of a culturally humble leader.

ACTIONS OF A CULTURALLY HUMBLE LEADER

Be Willing to Show Your Vulnerability

Self-awareness is one of the cornerstones of humility and hence cultural humility. This process involves understanding, recognizing, and acknowledging your strengths as well as your challenges. Acknowledgment for leaders is key because no one is perfect, and we are all prone to making mistakes. Malcolm Gladwell, author of *Talking to Strangers: What We Should Know about the People We Don't Know*, shared that he thought people were "longing for humility in our leaders today" (Winfrey, 2019, 0:31:04). Leaders must be self-revealing in terms of their capacity to work on their challenges and adapt their behaviors to improve their connection with those they are leading, and especially if they are from diverse cultures. Just being able to admit that you're wrong and moving forward from it is an extreme lesson in humility.

Use Your Authority to Promote and Acknowledge Others

Those who lead from humility understand the value of preparation, support, motivation, and promotion of their team as being the catalyst for success, whether it is from the perspective of a collective goal or a personal one. Micromanagement, for example, is not based in humility but could be rooted in insecurity and the need to be perfect. It demonstrates a lack of trust and an inability to delegate, thereby demotivating and discouraging independent decision-making. Micromanagers may tend to fall naturally into microaggression, which works against developing a culturally aware environment. Those who lead with humility understand the bigger picture—being able to see the forest through the empowerment of the vast variety of trees. Humility breeds humility.

Collaborate, Don't Compete!

"Success is better gained from a mindset of collaboration rather than competition" (Campbell, 2017, para 6). This is especially important when working with a diverse group of people with different backgrounds, identities, and motivations. Leaders who are undergirded in humility are not self-promoters but have the ability to build and maintain high-performing teams without the desire to compete with team members. Instead, they tend to take on more of a coaching position, seeing their role as helping each team member flourish in their competencies and expertise while also encouraging them to stretch from their comfort zones to seek growth and elevation. As humble leaders, they also encourage the team to bond and help each other, which builds cooperation, trust, and familiarity.

Team members should be encouraged to see difficult challenges as opportunities for growth and improvement without the burden of perceived penalty if not successful. Though healthy competition is often good from a sports perspective, as it allows teammates to learn from people who are more adept than they are, an overemphasis on competition in a library environment could create an unhealthy and toxic space leading to insecurities, jealousy, and fragmentation of the team. Leaders must be careful to not choose favorites and always walk in integrity, honesty, transparency, equity, fairness, competency, and gratitude. Humble leadership creates engagement and enables a team to perform more efficiently and effectively.

Work to Be Historically Aware

We all have our own belief systems, sets of values, and social norms that dictate the way we think, feel, and behave. "In order to practice true cultural humility, a person must also be aware of and sensitive to historic realities like legacies of violence and oppression against certain groups of people" (Sufrin, 2019, para 5). This is especially true for those in leadership. Oppressions, like racism and sexism, can manifest at different levels: ideological, institutional, interpersonal, and internal (Colorado Funders for Inclusiveness and Equity, 2010). The first three types of oppression conceptualize the basic premise that one group is better than another group and has the right to control the other. At the fourth level, the oppressed group internalizes negative messages about themselves that the dominant group has reflected interpersonally and through their institutions.

The U.S. Public Health Service's syphilis experiment at Tuskegee, the removal of cells from Henrietta Lacks without her knowledge, and experimentation by J. Marion Sims on enslaved Black women without the use of anesthesia are just a few of the many tragic examples of how Black Americans have been historically deprived of adequate health care and have suffered, all in the name of clinical research. This institutional distrust, abuse, and disrespect has led to skepticism about the purpose and research outcomes, which can be seen manifested today in the hesitancy of Black Americans to get COVID-19 vaccines.

By recognizing and acknowledging failures of the past, researchers, clinicians, providers, advocates, and other leaders can all contribute to building a better future that is rooted in practices of cultural humility.

Make Active Listening Your Habitual Friend

Leaders often feel that they must constantly be doing something to give them a sense of being in control. A very common mistake they make is to wrongly equate listening with passivity and subordination, so they tend to talk more (Geropp, 2020, para 18). Active listening requires the listener to concentrate and be fully attentive to what is being said so they can understand and respond appropriately. This important skill set should be habitual, becoming a natural part of the daily interaction and improving over time.

To build rapport and positively guide in an influential way, you must avoid the "mis" steps of not actively listening—misinterpretation, misunderstanding, misjudgment, misappropriation (unauthorized use without permission), misplacement (thoughts, feelings, actions), misdirection, and misbehavior, which can ultimately lead to mistakes and making misguided or wrong decisions. Though part of your role as a leader may be to project a sense of vision or purpose, you must be sure to actively listen to the members of your team in order to hear, acknowledge, and interpret the diverse voices and their concerns in their journey for buy-in and cooperation.

Be Willing to Follow

To be a good leader and exercise the actions previously described, you must first learn to be a good follower, as it humbles you and allows you to experience what it is like for others that you will lead. A notable quote from Aristotle (n.d.) says, "He who has never learned to obey cannot be a good commander." According to Sivers (2010), "It was the first follower that transformed the lone nut into a leader" (para 5). Good leaders inspire and motivate, whereas bad leaders divide, rule, and manipulate. As a result, it is highly unlikely that a bad leader, even if charismatic, will have any true followers because he cannot ask of others what he cannot or is unwilling to do himself. However, misplaced or excessive admiration of a bad leader can result in a cult following.

Having the ability to follow is critical especially in situations where you, as a leader, may need to defer your leadership stance to others who may have more expertise or differing opinions from yours. Many leaders have difficulty accepting other opinions and views if they don't match their own. However, "holding space is the soil for coaching" (Kim, 2019, para 12). When you hold space, you are open to other ideas, are willing to listen to feedback, and appreciate the strengths and contributions of others, thereby de-emphasizing yourself in order to emphasize someone else. When a person is not leading with humility, they may overwhelm the narrative with their own angles, views, wants, and needs, and instead of holding space, they grab it and sometimes disguise it as something else.

INTEGRATING CULTURAL HUMILITY INTO PRACTICE

Throughout the chapter, we use the word "leader" very broadly to include all individuals who assume some type of leadership role and on any level—whether it be work, home, or community. One does not need to have a big title or corner office to lead. Great leaders are intentional about being the best leaders possible for the people around them. They think strategically about the impact they want to have on people, the work they want to enable, and more importantly, what attributes are needed to cultivate and sustain an environment that elicits the best from the people they lead. Cable (2018) says, "No matter how long you've been in your role or how hard the journey was to get there—you are merely overhead unless you're bringing out the best in your employees. Unfortunately, many leaders lose sight of this" (para 1).

It is our hope that you will find the strategies outlined in this chapter to be applicable regardless of the context in which you are positioned. We challenge you to take action and lean into any discomfort you might feel when engaging in discussions on topics perceived to be difficult. Conversations about issues related to bias and the "isms" are often difficult to broach but very necessary to have. Adopting cultural humility as a practice will help you to not only navigate your environments but also engage people in ways that are respectful, healthy, and protective.

In a nutshell, this section encourages you to be active in integrating cultural humility into your practice by starting at the individual level, uncovering your biases, engaging in critical conversations, and committing to lifelong learning.

Starting at the Individual Level

Cultivating an environment where cultural humility is interwoven into the fabric of your personal or professional ecosystem starts at the individual level. It starts with you embarking on a process of intentional self-discovery. In your exploration to increase your awareness of self, you should consider your values, beliefs, predispositions, and upbringing. As individuals, we approach our work through the lens of our lived experiences, which gives us our frame of reference when approaching a new situation, encountering a challenge, trying to find a solution to a problem, or attempting to find common ground with a colleague, family member, or acquaintance.

"A frame of reference is a complex set of assumptions and attitudes which we use to filter perceptions to create meaning. The frame can include beliefs, schemas, preferences, values, culture and other ways in which we bias our understanding and judgment" (ChangingMinds.org, 2018, para 1). Each of us has a frame of reference that is enacted every waking moment of the day and influences the decisions we make throughout the day. More importantly, it is heavily influenced by the identities we hold. Therefore, it is impossible to discuss practicing cultural humility without first acknowledging the impact of identity.

Role of Identity and Intersectionality

Becoming self-aware requires a deep dive into diversity, equity, and inclusion (DEI) issues impacting the world and the people around us. Doing so requires leaders to embrace and respect the unique differences and identities they walk with every day, but more importantly, learning about the people they lead. Cultural humility is focused on learning about others. The definition of "diversity" from the Society of Human Resources Management (2020) says, "Diversity refers to the similarities and differences between individuals accounting for all aspects of one's personality and individual identity" (para 24). This definition emphasizes the importance of one's identity. Heshmat (2014) says, "Identity is largely concerned with the question: 'Who are you?' What does it mean to be who you are? Identity relates to our basic values that dictate the choices we make. These choices reflect who we are and what we value" (para 1). Understanding identity and how it is formed is of the utmost importance. Heshmat (2014) notes, "Very few people choose their identities. Instead, we simply internalize the values of our parents or the dominant cultures (e.g., the pursuit of materialism, power, and appearance)" (para 2).

The big eight social identifiers include ability, age, ethnicity, gender, race, religion, socioeconomic status/class, and sexual orientation. Each of these helps us understand who we are, and one's identity shapes the worldview that is embraced. Identity influences how individuals see, experience, respond, and interact in the world around them and impacts the decisions they make in the workplace. It is important that leaders take these things into consideration when striving to cultivate and sustain workplace environments that are inclusive.

Leaders who are aware of their own identity, as well as those around them, are better equipped to care for their followers. This increased awareness helps them to understand the concept of intersectionality and offers clarity in identifying the influences of power, privilege, and oppression in their environments. Legal scholar and civil rights activist Kimberlé Crenshaw coined the term "intersectionality" in 1989 "as a way to help explain the oppression of African-American women" (Columbia Law School, 2017, para 1). Now it is broadly used to describe how race, class, gender, socioeconomic status, physical or mental ability, age, immigrant status, and other social identities intersect with one another. The intersection of our identities creates privileges for some and oppressions for others. Ettarh (2018) notes,

> The experiences of a white queer patron (or librarian) will be very different from those of a black queer one. By treating these issues as separate entities, we as librarians fail to fully understand how oppressions work in various contexts. Intersectionality is a tool for studying, understanding, and responding to the ways in which axes of identities intersect and how these intersections contribute to unique experiences of oppression and privilege (para 2).

As individuals, we are complex, multilayered beings. To explore your identity, we encourage you to peel back those layers by considering the following questions:

- What identities do you hold?
- What are your personal values?
- How have your identities influenced your life or contributed to your professional success?

- When your identities intersect, what privileges or oppressions do they create for you?

When culturally humble leaders understand intersectionality, they notice when individuals in their environments are being marginalized, oppressed, sidelined, or silenced. More importantly, awareness of their own identities helps them to empathize with those they lead and move to action when harm has been caused or reported. Identity is the driving force behind biases (explicit and implicit) that we hold, and all of us have them.

Power and Privilege

There is a level of power and privilege that inherently comes with a leadership role. All leaders should be aware of and acknowledge how power and privilege impacts their leadership approach in their perspectives, their resonant voices, and their actions. They must be clear on how their own power and privilege frames their understanding of and relationships with the people they lead in their workplaces and how it is perceived by them. Unpacking power and privilege requires leaders to have a solid understanding of the definitions of both terms.

> **Power** is the possession of control, authority, or influence over others (Merriam-Webster, n.d.).
>
> **Privilege** is defined as "unearned access to resources (social power) that are only readily available to some people because of their social group membership; an advantage, or immunity granted to or enjoyed by one societal group above and beyond the common advantage of all other groups. Privilege is often invisible to those who have it (National Conference for Community and Justice, n.d.).

Questions for consideration when functioning as a culturally humble leader are:

- How am I using my privilege to help the people I lead?
- What power dynamics exist?
- How is power enacted in the library environment?

It is equally important for leaders to understand how they interact in the workplace and if any of their behaviors are causing oppression for the people around them.

> **Oppression** may be defined as "unjust or cruel exercise of authority or power." Oppression can occur on various levels via laws that work to keep

specific groups in power in which they continue to benefit, media representation or lack thereof, and the erasure of marginalized communities' history or voices (American Library Association, 2018).

When engaging in interactions, Mosher et al. (2017) say, a culturally humble leader might consider such questions as:

- What is it like to be this person?
- What is it about this person in front of me that makes them culturally unique?
- What aspects of this client's cultural background are important to them?
- How does this person's culture impact their reasons for attending counseling?
- How might this client's cultural context serve as a strength or support when working toward goals?
- How might this client's—and my own—cultural background impact our interaction and our ability to meaningfully connect and work together? (p. 224).

Considering these questions will likely position leaders to engage in critical conversations when cultures, beliefs, and perspectives collide. Answers could help leaders focus on how power and privilege may be impacting their environments and workforces and assist them in improving interactions with library patrons and staff alike.

Uncovering Your Biases

Adopting cultural humility requires critical reflection. Leaders who practice cultural humility are aware of their biases (explicit and implicit) and the impact they have on daily decisions they make. In general, biases are harmful, but it is implicit biases that are the most concerning. The Kirwan Institute (2012) defines implicit bias as "the attitudes or stereotypes that affect our understanding, actions, and decisions in an unconscious manner ... encompass both favorable and unfavorable assessments, are activated involuntarily and without an individual's awareness or intentional control" (para 1). Our brains are incredibly complex, and the implicit associations that we have formed are malleable, meaning they can be gradually unlearned through a variety of de-biasing techniques.

Implicit biases are just as pervasive in libraries as in other environments and could be evidenced in any of the following:

- interactions among the staff and with patrons
- recruitment process
- planning events or designing physical spaces
- allocating professional development funding

- acquiring materials for the collection
- developing and operationalizing policies
- committee appointments or nominations for awards
- library instruction

Leaders must be aware of what implicit biases look and sound like and have the tools to disrupt them in the moment. Everyone has biases, including individuals who champion DEI efforts in libraries. "Bias is a natural phenomenon in that our brains are constantly forming automatic associations as a way to better and more efficiently understand the world around us" (Kirwan Institute, n.d., 1).

The first step toward uncovering implicit biases is to take Harvard's Implicit Association Test (IAT), which measures attitudes and beliefs that people may be unwilling or unable to report (Project Implicit, 2011 para 2). While a complete erasure of biases is generally considered impossible, employing strategies like the IAT help mitigate implicit bias. Proximity to the people you lead should not be misconstrued as intimacy. Just because you work with someone does not necessarily give you insight into their life, their stories, or what they are dealing with. The benefit of uncovering your biases is that it will help you to see the library and the people you work with through new eyes. Listening with your eyes and ears may help increase your ability to look for visible cues of biases, allowing you to see whose voices are missing from the decision-making process.

A powerful leadership strategy for making the invisible visible is taking a momentary pause to reflect on conversations or situations that have occurred. Murdoch-Eaton and Sandars (2014) say, "Reflection is an essential aspect of all of our lives. We have an experience; we think about why we reacted in a certain way, and we then consider whether we need to take action and alter our response to similar experiences in the future" (p. 1).

Engaging in Difficult Conversations

As a leader you will need to engage in critical and difficult conversations on a variety of topics, which could be challenging for even the most seasoned leader. It is likely that the very thought of engaging in these conversations makes you feel uncomfortable, but we believe leaders must lean into discomfort and learn to be comfortable with being uncomfortable. When issues or challenges arise, the people you lead expect you to be prepared to pave the way for these conversations. Your engagement should display that you care just as much about them as you do about operationalizing the organization's mission.

Garfinkle (2017) encourages leaders to approach the difficult discussion with an open attitude and a genuine desire to learn. Knight (2015) shares, "Difficult conversations, whether you're telling a client the project is delayed or presiding over an unenthusiastic performance review, are an inevitable part of management" (para 1). The natural tendency is to avoid difficult conversations, but that is far from the solution. The reason why a conversation is needed will not go away with silence or avoidance. In fact, in some instances silence is perceived as complicity. Whatever problem or challenge you are facing will likely persist until you take action. Garfinkle (2017) says, "Avoiding or delaying a difficult conversation can hurt your relationships and create other negative outcomes" (para 1). To overcome any anxiety you might feel when engaging in a difficult conversation, Knight (2015) offers the following advice:

- Change your mindset by reframing it in a positive, less binary way.
- Take mindful breathing breaks throughout the day to refocus and build capacity to absorb any blows.
- Plan but don't script the conversation, remembering to be flexible as the conversation might veer off course.
- Acknowledge your counterpart's perspective by avoiding a *my-way-or-the-highway* attitude.
- Demonstrate compassion by delivering the difficult news in a courageous, honest, and fair way.
- Slow down and listen to ensure you are addressing the right issue and make sure your actions in that moment reinforce your words.
- Ask if there is something you can give back, especially if the conversation puts the other person in a difficult spot or takes something away from them.
- After the conversation, reflect and learn from the conversation by noting what went well and what did not go well, and consider what you would do differently.

Garfinkle (2017) reminds leaders to begin difficult conversations from a place of curiosity and respect. Approaching a conversation with the goal of being liked may lead to disastrous results in the long run. Other strategies offered include focusing on what you are hearing, not what you are preparing to say. Leaders must be direct in the conversation and should avoid filling it with information that is not related to the current discussion. Breaking the ice is one approach, but a focus on the present issue is the best strategy.

Garfinkle (2017) suggests getting right to the point with the goal of having an honest, respectful discussion where both parties speak frankly about the details of an issue. Being direct will look different for every leader, and how culture and personality impacts a person's comfort level should be considered. Leaders who do not value directness or whose culture or personality is conflict avoidant can still engage in difficult discussions by adjusting their approach.

> In these cases, shift your approach from overly direct to a respectful, affirming back-and-forth conversation. For instance, if the person you are talking with seems to not be picking up on what you are saying, ask them to repeat their understanding of what you've shared. As they reflect back

what they've heard, you can adjust your message to make sure the conflict is moving toward resolution. This communication style is open and less threatening. (Garfinkel, 2017, para 6)

We live in a world where hate speech and cancel culture have been normalized, stories of police brutality are in constant rotation on the national news, and Black and Brown communities are impacted by a variety of issues at disproportionate rates throughout the United States. In *Hateful Conduct in Libraries: Supporting Library Workers and Patrons*, the ALA (2018) offers guidance to library workers who plan to initiate conversations among staff members and within their communities. The guide is divided into three sections, anchored by the perspectives below with questions categorized as:

1. Proactive Preparation (What strategic steps can I take to prepare in the event hateful conduct situations occur within the library?)
2. Responding to an Incident (What do I do if hateful conduct is directed at me, a colleague, or a patron, and how do I follow up?)
3. Meeting Community Needs (How do I balance access to all viewpoints while also identifying and supporting historically marginalized perspectives?) (para 3).

Integrating cultural humility into practice requires leaders to engage meaningfully and courageously, finding common ground through conversation. In his book *Black Man in a White Coat*, Dr. Damon Tweedy shared that a measure of his success in psychiatry was due to his ability to find common ground with patients by talking with them through the lens of his lived experiences. In her 2018 TED Talk, Julia Dhar offers strategies for disagreeing productively and finding common ground. She says:

People who disagree the most productively start by finding common ground, no matter how narrow it is. They identify the thing that we can all agree on and go from there: the right to an education, equality between all people, the importance of safer communities. What they're doing is inviting us into what psychologists call shared reality. And shared reality is the antidote to alternative facts. (Dhar, 2018, 03:01)

Engaging in difficult conversations, especially ones focused on addressing issues related to social identities, is not a skill that leaders develop overnight. It involves a healthy combination of practice balanced with a mixture of compassion, empathy, courage, and humility. Becoming a culturally humble leader who can meet the challenge of engaging in difficult conversations is a lifelong endeavor. Though it is likely to get better over time, we encourage you to take action to learn and improve your effectiveness in communicating and engaging with people from different backgrounds and cultures.

Being a Lifelong Learner

A popular quote attributed to Maya Angelou says, "Do the best you can until you know better. Then when you know better, do better" ("Quotable Quote by Maya Angelou," n.d.). Doing better is an active, iterative process without an endpoint. Culturally humble practitioners are lifelong learners who operate with curiosity, openness, and a willingness to make mistakes. Those who lead with cultural humility are constantly working to sharpen their skills to become better leaders. An effective leader constantly works on improving his or her leadership skills. If you are not learning, you are not growing. Fortunately, we encounter people and situations that push us to challenge our thinking and perspectives, often resulting in a change in practice. Walters and Asbill (2013) say:

> We never arrive at a point where we are done learning. Therefore, we must be humble and flexible, bold enough to look at ourselves critically and desire to learn more. When we do not know something, are we able to say that we do not know? Willingness to act on the acknowledgement that we have not and will not arrive at a finish line is integral to this aspect of cultural humility as well. Understanding is only as powerful as the action that follows. (para 3)

Hughes et al. (2020) offer a variety of practical strategies, many of which can be applied in library environments, used for teaching cultural humility to health-care students. The strategies offered are on the intrapersonal, interpersonal, and system levels. The authors note that it is impossible to provide an exhaustive list of best practices, because increasing one's cultural humility is "both a goal and a process, as such those striving towards it have to constantly evaluate their progress and identify alternative approaches to reach that goal" (Hughes et al., 2020, 32). Example strategy levels include:

1. Intrapersonal: Intentionally engage in self-critique and reflexivity to recognize and accept biases and assumptions.
2. Interpersonal: Engage in mindful active listening where clinicians ask genuine open-ended questions of the people they encounter to understand their cultural beliefs and practices.
3. System: Offer opportunities for individual self-critique and reflexivity during paid work time, offer workshops and space for discussion, and engage in community participatory approaches to develop policies that build a culture of humility (pp. 31–32).

There is no single best strategy for increasing cultural humility, but a good place to start is by investigating the variety of resources available on the topic. There is no shortage of items available to read, watch, or complete related to cultural humility. A simple Google search for the phrase "cultural humility" yields thousands of results for books, articles, and other resources, and Amazon and YouTube searches will be just as fruitful. There are a variety of webinars and online training sessions/videos/modules available, many for free, due in part to people working from home as a consequence of the pandemic. Culturally humble leaders should be able to easily identify and access resources to support their individual learning needs.

After you find a few good resources to digest, we encourage you to take action. Mosher et al. (2017) say culturally humble leaders intentionally self-reflect and make a consistent effort to reduce their limitations and biases;

A. focus on learning from their clients' cultural backgrounds and experiences;
B. search for opportunities to build respectful, mutual partnerships with their clients; and
C. are motivated throughout their lives to learn more about various cultural beliefs (p. 224).

CONCLUSION

Self-reflection and self-critique are the root of cultural humility. This chapter explored cultural humility in the context of leadership, unpacking what it should look like in everyday practice.

The authors defined "leader" in this chapter very broadly to include all individuals who assume some type of leadership role and on any level—whether it be work, home, business, organization, or community. However, those who lead with humility understand the value of preparation, support, motivation, and promotion of their team as being the catalyst for success, whether it is from the perspective of a shared goal or a personal one.

This chapter has shared lessons learned from activating and experiencing humility in leadership approaches, focusing on three areas. It is critical to first understand *why practicing cultural humility is important*, which can be attributed primarily to the dominance and pervasiveness of societal "isms," along with increasing diversity and its competitive advantage. Both factors are dictating why it is important that we take action toward integrating cultural humility into our daily practice. Humility in leadership feeds overall effectiveness, so the *actions of a culturally humble leader*, from showing vulnerability to being willing to follow first, are crucial to the effectiveness in communicating and engaging with people from different backgrounds and cultures. *Integrating cultural humility into practice* starts at the individual level with reflecting on identity, intersectionality, and biases and culminates with the desire to be a lifelong learner. Effective leaders are always a perpetual work in progress.

REFERENCES

American Library Association. (2018). *Hateful conduct in libraries: Supporting library workers and patrons.*

Aristotle Quotes. (n.d.) Citatis.com.

Boesen, L. (2012, January 17). Creating connections through cultural humility. http://www.lisaboesen.com/creating-connections-through-cultural-humility/

Cable, D. (2018, April 23). How humble leadership really works. *Harvard Business Review.*

Campbell, S. (2017). *9 reasons humility is the key ingredient to exceptional leadership.* Entrepreneur.

ChangingMinds.org. *Frame of reference.* Retrieved February 21, 2021, from https://changingminds.org/explanations/models/frame_of_reference.htm

Colorado Funders for Inclusiveness and Equity. (2010). *The four "I's" of oppression.* http://www.coloradoinclusivefunders.org/uploads/1/1/5/0/11506731/the_four_is_of_oppression.pdf

Columbia Law School. (2017). *Kimberlé Crenshaw on intersectionality, more than two decades later.* https://www.law.columbia.edu/news/archive/kimberle-crenshaw-intersectionality-more-two-decades-later

Dhar, J. (2018, October). *How to disagree productively and find common ground.* [Video]. https://www.ted.com/talks/julia_dhar_how_to_disagree_productively_and_find_common_ground

Ettarh, F. (2018). *Vocational awe and librarianship: The lies we tell ourselves.* In the Library with the Lead Pipe. https://www.inthelibrarywiththeleadpipe.org/2018/vocational-awe/

Frey, W. H. (2018). *US will become "minority white" in 2045, Census projects.* Bookings.

Garfinkle, J. (2017, May 24,). *How to have difficult conversations when you don't like conflict.* Harvard Business Review. https://hbr.org/2017/05/how-to-have-difficult-conversations-when-you-dont-like-conflict

Geropp, B. (2020). *Leadership mistakes! The top ten and how to avoid them!* https://www.berndgeropp.com/leadership-mistakes/

Gladwell, M. (2019). *Talking to strangers: What we should know about the people we don't know.* Allen Lane.

Heshmat, S. (2014). *Basics of identity.* Psychology Today. http://www.psychologytoday.com/blog/science-choice/201412/basics-identity

Hodge, T. (2019). Integrating cultural humility into public services librarianship. *The International Information & Library Review, 51*(3), 268–274. https://doi.org/10.1080/10572317.2019.1629070

Hook, J. N., Davis, D. E., Owen, J., Worthington, E. L., & Utsey, S. O. (2013). Cultural humility: Measuring openness to culturally diverse clients. *Journal of Counseling Psychology, 60*(3), 353–366. https://doi.org/10.1037/a0032595

Hughes, V., Delva, S., Nkimbeng, M., Spaulding, E., Turkson-Ocran, R., Cudjoe, J., Ford, A., Rushton, C., DAoust, R., & Han, H. (2020). Not missing the opportunity: Strategies to promote cultural humility among future nursing faculty. *Journal of Professional Nursing, 36*(1), 28–33. https://doi.org/10.1016/j.profnurs.2019.06.005

Introduction to the human resources discipline of diversity, equity and inclusion. (2020). SHRM. https://www.shrm.org/resourcesandtools/tools-and-samples/toolkits/pages/introdiversity.aspx

Kim, J. (2019). *What does it mean/look like to hold space for someone?* Psychology Today. https://www.psychologytoday.com/blog/the-angry-therapist/201910/what-does-it-meanlook-hold-space-someone

Kirwan Institute. (n.d). *What is implicit bias?* Ohio State University. http://kirwaninstitute.osu.edu/implicit-bias-training/resources/mythbusters.pdf

Kirwan Institute. (2012). *Understanding implicit bias.* Ohio State University. https://kirwaninstitute.osu.edu/article/understanding-implicit-bias

Knight, R. (2015, January 9). *How to handle difficult conversations at work.* Harvard Business Review. https://hbr.org/2015/01/how-to-handle-difficult-conversations-at-work

Merriam-Webster. (n.d.) *Definition of power.* https://www.merriam-webster.com/dictionary/power

Mosher, D. K., Hook, J. N., Captari, L. E., Davis, D. E., DeBlaere, C., & Owen, J. (2017). Cultural humility: A therapeutic framework for engaging diverse clients. *Practice Innovations (Washington, D.C.), 2*(4), 221–233. https://doi.org/10.1037/pri0000055

Murdoch-Eaton, D., & Sandars, J. (2014). Reflection: moving from a mandatory ritual to meaningful professional development. *Archives of Disease in Childhood, 99*(3), 279–283. https://doi.org/10.1136/archdischild-2013-303948

National Conference for Community and Justice. (n.d.) *Social Justice Definitions.* https://www.nccj.org/resources/social-justice-definitions

Phillips, K. W. (2014). *How diversity makes us smarter.* Scientific American. https://www.scientificamerican.com/article/how-diversity-makes-us-smarter/

Project Implicit. (n.d.). *Education, overview: Implicit Association Test (IAT).* https://implicit.harvard.edu/implicit/education.html

"Quotable Quote by Maya Angelou." (n.d.) Goodreads.com. https://www.goodreads.com/quotes/7273813-do-the-best-you-can-until-you-know-better-then

Riggers, D. (2018). *How a diverse workforce can be your competitive advantage.* https://www.hcamag.com/au/news/opinion-and-best-practice/how-a-diverse-workforce-can-be-your-competitive-advantage/151865

Rodriguez, E. (2020). Diversity and inclusion in libraries: A call to action and strategies for success. *Public Services Quarterly, 16*(1), 27–28. https://doi.org/10.1080/15228959.2019.1696991

Society of Human Resources Management. (2020). *Introduction to the human resources discipline of diversity, equity and inclusion.* SHRM. https://www.shrm.org/resourcesandtools/tools-and-samples/toolkits/pages/introdiversity.aspx

Sivers, D. (2010). *First follower: Leadership lessons from a dancing guy.* https://www.paragonpd.com/latest-news/41-first-follower-leadership-lessons-from-a-dancing-guy

Sufrin, J. (2019, November 5). *3 things to know: Cultural humility.* Hogg Foundation for Mental Health, University of Texas at Austin. https://hogg.utexas.edu/3-things-to-know-cultural-humility

Tervalon, M., & Murray-García, J. (1998). Cultural humility versus cultural competence: A critical distinction in defining physician training outcomes in multicultural education. *Journal of Health Care for the Poor and Underserved, 9*(2), 117–125. https://doi.org/10.1353/hpu.2010.0233

Walters, A., & Asbill, L. (2013). *Reflections on cultural humility.* American Psychological Association. https://www.apa.org/pi/families/resources/newsletter/2013/08/cultural-humility

Winfrey, O. (Host). (2019, September 18). *Malcolm Gladwell: Talking to Strangers* [Audio podcast]. SuperSoul Conversations. https://omny.fm/shows/oprah-s-supersoul-conversations/malcolm-gladwell-talking-to-strangers

10

Professional Development for Cultural Humility

Tish Hayes

Cultural humility is a promising approach to diversity, equity, and inclusion work within libraries. The focus on self-reflection, lifelong learning and growth, and commitment to taking action within one's own personal context and community reflects many of the values that librarianship centers as articulated in the American Library Association's (ALA) Core Values of Librarianship, including democracy, diversity, education and lifelong learning, the public good, service, and social responsibility. Cultural humility urges us to embrace the complexities of ourselves and our communities, challenging librarians to reconsider the idea of competence, which emphasizes sufficiency and efficiency. This shift might begin in an individual but must be moved along by organizational and institutional investment. Through ongoing scaffolded training, professional development can support academic library workers in implementing cultural humility as a personal and professional practice. The work of individuals to cultivate cultural humility is the first step in transforming institutions and creating more equitable and inclusive libraries. This chapter will provide an overview of the value of cultural humility as a foundation for diversity, equity, and inclusion (DEI) work and focus on the importance of personal and institutional commitments to cultural humility. It will offer topical examples and resources for implementing professional development that fosters cultural humility.

THE LIMITS OF COMPETENCE

Despite decades of diversity initiatives, the predominant whiteness within the field of librarianship was 86.7 percent at the last official count (ALA Office of Research and Statistics Demographic Study Report, 2017). This often results in library faculty and staff at academic institutions not fully representing the diverse student populations that utilize library spaces, resources, and services. This lack of racial diversity also impacts the faculty and staff of color employed in libraries, resulting in additional emotional labor, low morale (Kendrick, 2017), microaggressions, and other forms of a hostile work environment. Creating equitable and inclusive libraries requires that library staff work to redress harms perpetuated by individuals and the systems that uphold the values of white supremacy.

The Association of College and Research Libraries (ACRL) developed a set of diversity standards in 2012 detailing the skills and actions of culturally competent librarians and library staff. The Racial and Ethnic Diversity Committee of ACRL based the standards on the 2001 National Association of Social Workers Standards for Cultural Competence in Social Work Practice, adopting their definition of cultural competence:

> A congruent set of behaviors, attitudes, and policies that enable a person or group to work effectively in cross-cultural situations; the process by which individuals and systems respond respectfully and effectively to people of all cultures, languages, classes, races, ethnic backgrounds, religions, and other diversity factors in a manner that recognizes, affirms, and values the worth of individuals, families, and communities and protects and preserves the dignity of each.

This definition of cultural competence implies that creating an equitable and inclusive library rests on acquiring and applying a particular set of knowledge and skills. Professional development focused on cultural competence often highlights unique characteristics of cultures to recognize and understand differences. Although these kinds of workshops are intended to equip library workers with cultural information to serve their communities better, an unintended consequence may be the marginalization of cultures that are not the dominant culture (white, Christian, hetero, cis, able-bodied, etc.).

Another concern with focusing professional development efforts on cultural competence is that changing "behaviors, attitudes, and policies" (ACRL) is often seen as a linear process with a clear start and end point (Fisher-Borne et al., 2015). This approach does not consider the complexities of identity or the ongoing, lifelong process of learning and unlearning cultural biases and norms. The idea of competence also encourages library workers to think of themselves as knowledgeable about cultural practices that may not be their own while discounting the power structures that impact different communities.

CULTURAL HUMILITY AS A DISTINCT FRAMEWORK

The medical and social work literature has documented the movement away from cultural competence and toward cultural humility. Cultural humility is a framework distinct from cultural competence that focuses on self-reflection, lifelong learning, and ongoing engagement in community rather than acquiring cultural information to become knowledgeable or competent (Tervalon & Murray-Garcia, 1998). In a concept analysis, Foronda et al. (2015) identify the attributes of cultural humility as "openness, self-awareness, egoless, supportive interaction, and self-reflection and critique" (pp. 2–3).

Our identities and those of our patrons are complex, and the impact of structural oppression presents differently across these identities. The complexity of identities will not likely be seen within the scope of a reference transaction or an instruction session. As library workers, we cannot make assumptions about the salience of the many identities of our patrons and colleagues. "Intersectionality" was coined by Kimberlé Crenshaw in 1998 and is defined in Merriam-Webster as "the complex, cumulative way in which the effects of multiple forms of discrimination (such as racism, sexism, and classism) combine, overlap, or intersect especially in the experiences of marginalized individuals or groups." It is an important concept in understanding the value of cultural humility, which offers "an alternative approach that focuses on knowledge of self in relation to others, acknowledges the dynamic nature of culture, and challenges barriers that impact marginalized communities on both individual and institutional levels" (Fisher-Borne et al., 2015, 171). This shift from knowledge about others to knowledge about ourselves and our positionality is significant, as is the imperative to explicitly address systems of oppression.

DEVELOPING CULTURAL HUMILITY WITHIN THE PROFESSION

Professional development for librarians and other library workers is built into the structure of our professional organizations at the national, state, and local levels. The ACRL issued a statement in 2000 on professional development that emphasized the importance of a commitment to professional excellence, and that pursuit is an individual one that should be supported institutionally. While the statement acknowledges rapid technological changes as a driving force of the focus on lifelong learning and adaptation, it does not provide guidance on what kinds of professional development should be prioritized or best practices for delivery.

What constitutes professional development is often in the eye of the beholder and may range from conference attendance to reading groups within the library (Sobczak & Bradshaw, 2017). The range of activities and topics available for professional development is often determined by the type of institution and one's role within the library. Many academic institutions include professional development for librarians as part of a budget or as a benefit or negotiated salary. These opportunities are not always available to other workers within the library, either due to budget or scheduling constraints. These limitations must be addressed when considering cultural humility as a framework for creating equitable and inclusive libraries.

Cultivating cultural humility requires a practice of self-reflection among all library staff and a shared understanding of how power and privilege impact relationships within the library and with the communities we serve. Professional development to support a cultural humility framework should be ongoing and inclusive of all library workers, including part-time staff and student workers who often have limited access to such opportunities. The positionality of workers should also be considered when designing professional development. Conversations about cultural humility still center dominant groups in an overwhelmingly white profession. Hurley et al. (2019) point out that the big idea behind any inclusive training is that "my norms are not the only norms, and unfamiliar norms are not necessarily wrong" (p. 11), which is often a transformative concept for white people but may already be a fundamental understanding for marginalized communities.

Professional development should also be ongoing and integrated into the expectations and resources provided to library workers. Cultural humility cannot be accomplished in a workshop; instead, it is an ongoing process of self-awareness and skill development requiring action on the part of the individual and support from the institution.

CULTURAL HUMILITY TOPICS FOR PROFESSIONAL DEVELOPMENT

The impact of implicit bias in workplaces has been well documented (Alabi, 2018; Dalton, & Villagran, 2018; Cooke & Sweeney, 2019) and training to minimize implicit bias has become a common component of diversity, equity, and inclusion workshops. A good starting point for professional development in this area would be for staff to take one or more of the Implicit Association Tests (IAT) from Project Implicit (Project Implicit, 2011). These tests help individuals recognize attitudes and beliefs they may not realize they have. The IAT website provides examples of different kinds of implicit biases related to gender, race, class, etc. These biases often reflect stereotypes that will seem familiar, like assuming a doctor or scientist is a man rather than a woman. Even if we reject these stereotypes, the biases they come from are often deeply embedded in our unconscious minds (Project Implicit, 2011).

Taking these IAT tests may create discomfort and reveal aspects of ourselves that are not flattering. In a professional context, this level of vulnerability may feel unsettling. However, avoiding implicit biases, those unconscious and automatic responses that impact our work and relationships, ensures the status quo of an inequitable and potentially harmful library culture (Hodge, 2019). Taking the tests, spending time in self-reflection to reckon with difficult truths, and creating opportunities to discuss implicit biases identified through the tests is an important first step. Ultimately, this kind of professional development aims to inspire action and facilitate change. Recognizing how our implicit biases show up in library policies, collections, hiring, and communication should be the next step in creating more equitable practices and systems.

Identity work is another area to consider for professional development in cultural humility. Creating workshops that provide time for library staff to reflect on the various components of their identities (race, class, gender, sexuality, religious affiliation, etc.) can help them recognize their positionality: "the notion that personal values, views, and location in time and space influence how one understands the world. In this context, gender, race, class, and other aspects of identities are indicators of social and spatial positions and are not fixed, given qualities" (Warf, 2010). This reflection must consider which aspects of our identities are most salient, how those identities impact our understanding of ourselves, and what power and privilege those identities afford us. The Power Flower is a good tool for reflecting on our personal and social identities and beginning a conversation about positionality.

The Power Flower was first presented in *Educating for a Change* (1991) as a way to "identify who we are (and who we aren't) as individuals and as a group in relation to those who wield power in our society" (p. 87). Each person is given a worksheet with a flower drawn on it. The center of the flower, which should be surrounded by two rings of petals, is divided into sixteen sections, each labeled with a different social identity (race, class, gender identity, etc.). Each participant should fill in the inner set of petals with their identity, and the outer petals should be labeled with the dominant identity (the identity with the most social power). As participants reflect on how their identities do or do not match with the dominant identities, there is an opportunity to discuss social power, intersectionality, the impact their identities have on the way they see the world, and how they interact with each other and their patrons. Many organizations have adapted and shared their versions of the Power Flower with reflection and discussion questions. A guided course, intended to be used with pairs or a group, is offered through the Freedom Lifted Learning Lab. Any of these resources can be readily located through a Google search.

DELIVERY OF PROFESSIONAL DEVELOPMENT FOR CULTURAL HUMILITY

Professional development can be implemented in different ways, and that variety will be useful in reaching the widest range of library workers across many identities.

Affinity groups, also known as employee resource groups (ERGs), are formed by employees around a shared issue or identity. They can offer space for staff to connect and discuss common interests and concerns in a safe environment. While affinity groups are often considered to be beneficial in promoting social ties and feelings of belonging, more recent iterations of ERGs also focus on mentorship and career advancement. These groups may offer leadership in cultural humility professional development, as well as insight into DEI areas that need to be addressed by the institution. A recent McKinsey report (Catalino et al., 2022) found that ERGs are most effective when integrated with the larger institution's DEI goals, once again reiterating the importance of institutional support of professional development for cultural humility initiatives.

Most professional development will require people of different identities and perspectives to meet and discuss cultural humility concepts across these differences. Creating a "brave space" (Arao & Clemens, 2013) for participants to have challenging conversations should be considered with any professional development offering. Creating group agreements is one way to prepare for those online or in-person conversations and set participants up for success.

Group agreements are ideas and actions that participants accept as essential for creating an environment that invites generative conversations about diversity, equity, and inclusion, as well as the openness required for cultural humility. The Anti-Oppression Resource and Training Alliance (AORTA) and the Equity Lab both offer examples that are useful starting points. Many agreements will be common across professional development activities, though each workshop or webinar might need to adjust the agreements based on the participants or topics. Group agreements like "acknowledging the difference between intent and impact" and "move up, move up" into a speaking or listening role (AORTA, 2017) act as guidelines for engagement and work as reminders to everyone in the room to be attentive to power dynamics. Rather than rules imposed by a leader or human resources, group agreements are co-created to support and encourage each person in the room to participate fully.

Small-group discussions centering on relevant articles or texts are easy starting points for professional development. These kinds of discussions can be initiated at any library staff level, even without the support of a supervisor. Examining articles offers an opportunity for learning and serves as a foundation for conversation. Ideas expressed in the text can then be connected to what is happening in the library, participants' lives, and the community. This kind of professional development might be a casual conversation between two to three colleagues or a more formalized group discussion at the department, library, or consortia level.

In-person or online interactive workshops offer the opportunity to focus on particular concepts or issues that will be impactful for attendees. They can be an excellent start to a longer, more sustained campaign around an issue. Workshops can also be a space where colleagues can engage in ways that are different from traditional work roles. They should be scaffolded to ensure that all participants can fully engage with the content and each other.

Many academic workplaces have DEI training available to employees, which can build a foundation for workshops specific to library staff and with a focus on cultural humility. Establishing connections with the campus DEI office or organizational leaders for ideas, resources, and support can foster ongoing relationships that contribute to the growth of cultural humility capacity. YouTube and TED Talks are a free and easy way to access resources for professional development. For example, the San José State University School of Information hosts a free diversity series on YouTube, which includes the presentation "Integrating Cultural Humility into Librarianship." TED Talks also provides curated content organized into thematic playlists, including topics like diversity and inclusion.

An increasing number of online courses are dedicated to either cultural humility or topics that encourage the development of cultural humility.

- The American Library Association offers in-person and online training through the Office for Diversity, Literacy, and Outreach Services (ODLOS) (https://www.ala.org/aboutala/offices/diversity). ODLOS also provides a list of equity, diversity, and inclusion programming geared toward librarians.
- DeEtta Jones and Associates (https://www.deettajones.com) is a consulting firm owned by a Black woman that offers training on equity, diversity, and inclusion as well as strategy development.
- Library Juice Academy (https://libraryjuiceacademy.com/) has several courses that can be completed to gain a Certificate of Diversity and Inclusion Skills.
- We Here (https://www.wehere.space/), a professional organization created by and for people of color working in libraries, offers workshops and classes that center anti-racist pedagogy.

Training from the Library Juice Academy, ODLOS, DeEtta Jones and Associates, and We Here all require a financial commitment. Individual librarians might be encouraged to use professional development funds for these opportunities, but making the training available to all staff shows the institutional investment in cultural humility and workplace equity initiatives.

CONCLUSION

While professional development can be pursued on an individual basis, real transformation occurs when the institution commits to cultural humility by allocating resources and time to ensure that all staff benefit from professional development opportunities. Professional development is just the first step, and it must be followed by the leadership of academic libraries supporting the changes in policies, services, and collections that will ensue.

REFERENCES

ALA Office of Research and Statistics Demographic Study Report. (2017). https://www.ala.org/tools/sites/ala.org.tools/files/content/Draft%20of%20Member%20Demographics%20Survey%2001-11-2017.pdf

Alabi, J. (2018). From hostile to inclusive: Strategies for improving the racial climate of academic libraries. *Library Trends, 67*(1), 131–146. doi:10.1353/lib.2018.0029.

AORTA. (2017). *Anti-oppressive facilitation for democratic process.* https://arts-campout-2015.sites.olt.ubc.ca/files/2019/02/AORTA_Facilitation-Resource-Sheet-JUNE2017.pdf

Arao, B. & Clemens, K. (2013). From safe spaces to brave spaces: A new way to frame dialogue around diversity and social justice. In L. Landreman (ed.), *The art of effective facilitation* (pp. 135–150). Stylus.

Association of College and Research Libraries. (2000). Statement on professional development. *College & Research Libraries News, 61* (10), 933–937. https://doi.org/10.5860/crln.61.10.933

Catalino, N., Gardner, N., Goldstein, D., & Wong, J. (2022, December 7). *Effective employee resource groups are key to inclusion at work. Here's how to get them right.* McKinsey & Company. https://www.mckinsey.com/capabilities/people-and-organizational-performance/our-insights/effective-employee-resource-groups-are-key-to-inclusion-at-work-heres-how-to-get-them-right

Cooke, N. A. & Sweeney, M. E. (2019). Implicit bias and microaggressions in library and information science. In S. D. Jones & B. Murphy (eds.), *Diversity and inclusion in libraries: A call to action and strategies for success* (pp. 35–41). Rowman & Littlefield.

Dalton, S., & Villagran, M. (2018). Minimizing and addressing implicit bias in the workplace: Be proactive, part one. *College & Research Libraries News, 79*(9), 478. doi:https://doi.org/10.5860/crln.79.9.478

Fisher-Borne, M., Cain, J. M., & Martin, S. L. (2015). From mastery to accountability: Cultural humility as an alternative to cultural competence. *Social Work Education, 34*(2), 165–181. http://dx.doi.org/10.1080/02615479.2014.977244

Foronda, C., Baptiste, D. L., Reinholdt, M. M., & Ousman, K. (2015). Cultural humility: A concept analysis. *Journal of Transcultural Nursing: Official Journal of the Transcultural Nursing Society, 27*(3), 210–217. https://doi.org/10.1177/1043659615592677

Hodge, T. (2019). Integrating cultural humility into public services librarianship. *International Information & Library Review, 51*(3), 268–274. DOI: 10.1080/10572317.2019.1629070

Hurley, D. A., Kostelecky, S. R. and Townsend, L. (2019), Cultural humility in libraries. *Reference Services Review, 47*(4), 544–555. https://doi.org/10.1108/RSR-06-2019-0042

Kendrick, K. D. (2017). The low morale experience of academic librarians: A phenomenological study. *Journal of Library Administration, 57*(8), 846–878. DOI: 10.1080/01930826.2017.1368325

Project Implicit. (2011). https://www.projectimplicit.net/

Sobczak, P. D. & Bradshaw, K. (2017). Professional development in libraries: One size does not fit all. Proceedings of the Charleston Library Conference. http://dx.doi.org/10.5703/1288284316674

Tervalon, M., & Murray-Garcia, J. (1998). Cultural humility versus cultural competence: A critical distinction in defining physician training outcomes in multicultural education. *Journal of Health Care for the Poor and Underserved, 9*(2), 117–125.

Warf, B. (2010). Positionality. In *Encyclopedia of geography* (vol. 1, p. 2258). SAGE Publications. https://dx.doi.org/10.4135/9781412939591.n913

Part III

Voices from the Field

11

Using Your Power(s) for Good

THOUGHTS ON POWER, PRIVILEGE, AND CULTURAL HUMILITY

Gina R. Costello

This chapter explores the concepts of power and privilege in the context of equity, diversity, and inclusion (EDI). Cultural humility provides a framework for exploring ways that individual and institutional privilege perpetuate inequities that stymie EDI efforts in library and information science (LIS). The discussion will focus on whiteness because that is part of my identity, with an acknowledgment that privilege and power are relative and intersectional.

If you are reading this and you are white, it is likely that you may also identify as female, cisgender, able-bodied, and middle-class. If many or all of these identifiers apply to you, then you are in the majority of LIS professionals. If you do not describe yourself with these identifiers, you are likely aware that they *do* describe most individuals working in the LIS field.

According to the U.S. household data annual averages report (U.S. Bureau of Labor Statistics, 2020), over 86 percent of the LIS workforce is white, and nearly 80 percent are women. Lack of diversity in LIS has been recognized in the literature for decades (Brook et al., 2016), and a variety of efforts are underway to provide more opportunities for traditionally underrepresented and marginalized groups to enter and succeed in the profession. Despite good efforts in this area, *Cultural Proficiencies for Racial Equity* (2022), coauthored by members of the American Library Association (ALA) and the Association of Research Libraries (ARL), identifies the inadequacy of diversity and minority recruitment efforts in LIS, noting that they are doing little more than maintaining the current numbers of nonwhite LIS professionals.

When diversity is framed as a problem to be solved, Galvan (2015) contends that the responsibility and outcomes are placed on underrepresented and marginalized groups to conform to the white ideals of the profession. Sierpe (2019) asserts that "underrepresentation is simply a visible symptom of a much larger problem: librarianship as a system whose existential function is to preserve, manage, and defend a structure for informational, educational, cultural and political race-based domination" (p. 86). Acknowledging that LIS has much to do with EDI, practicing cultural humility is a way to approach social justice issues that have gained traction in fields such as social work and psychology.

Over the past few years, I have heard white people in LIS lament about what they see as an overemphasis on equity, diversity, and inclusion initiatives. These individuals may be reluctant to acknowledge that only the privilege and power of their positions allow them to make these criticisms. I admit that I have agreed in some instances that EDI issues have sometimes eclipsed other topics. However, I realize that whether I feel comfortable, neutral, supportive, engaged, or angry, it is my responsibility as a leader and as part of the dominant group to decenter my feelings and use whatever power I have for good. No matter how I feel, I need to embrace a mindset that nothing will change unless those in power make strong statements supporting diversity.

ORDINARY PRIVILEGE

If, like me, you are part of the LIS white female majority, you hold privilege and power in your workplace and the profession. We have what Chugh (2018) called "ordinary privilege," because "it blends in with the norms and people around us and is easily forgotten" (para 2). In the seminal work "White Privilege: Unpacking the Invisible Knapsack," McIntosh (1989) wrote, "White Privilege is like an invisible weightless knapsack of special provisions, maps, passports, codebooks, visas, clothes, tools and blank checks" (p. 95). Privilege is a right, benefit, or advantage conferred on a group or individual not because of something they did or failed to do but simply for being part of that group (McIntosh, 1989).

Identities that can give an individual or group privilege include gender, race, religion, sexual orientation, country of origin, language, ability, and socioeconomic status. Privilege does not make one immune to hardship; however, it does give an unearned advantage or benefit (Ebbitt, 2015). Being privileged doesn't necessarily determine how successful one will be, but it does make it more likely that whatever abilities, talents, or ambitions one has will result in a good outcome (Johnson, 2017). In *Diversity beyond Lip Service* (2019), La'Wana Harris encourages us to question our relationship with privilege, identify the role it has in our career development, examine how it affects nonmajority employees in our organization, and interrogate our own biases.

Most people have some ordinary privilege, which is not something we should be ashamed of or deny. Acknowledging and owning one's privilege is key to addressing societal imbalances. Norman and Adelman (2022) recommend reframing the concept from "owning our privilege" to "working from our privileged identities" (para 4). They suggest that working from our privileged identities to help those with marginalized identities can reveal our "learning edges (places where what we are consciously aware and actively addressing our own personal journey and leave room for others to join in the process from their own perspectives" (Norman & Adelman, 2022, para 5). The process of being more aware of one's privilege should not be viewed as a burden or source of guilt but instead as an opportunity to learn and take responsibility while working to make a more inclusive and equitable world.

ACKNOWLEDGING POWER AND PRIVILEGE

I believe change begins with an individual journey that is meant to be challenging, illuminating, and ongoing. Such personal journeys should be shared whenever possible to dispel ignorance, improve understanding, and empower others whenever possible. Too many of us with power and privilege do not name the issues outright. We do not talk about this challenging topic. Perhaps many of us are unaware of our privilege until a catalyst or life event pushes us to see the invisible force. For these reasons, I share some of my journey.

I identify as a white cisgender heterosexual woman who has lived a middle-class life in the southeastern United States for all my forty-seven years. Various advantages that I did not earn ensured that I could attend a college-preparatory high school and a private college. Even later when I attended graduate school part-time while working full-time low-paying jobs, I had the safety net of my parents and in-laws. Though my parents were not wealthy, they valued higher education and made sacrifices so that I could have opportunities.

I am married and the parent of two children who benefit from my privilege. My older daughter, now a teenager, has special needs that will prevent her from being able to live independently. Her differences since birth have presented challenges to my family; however, I acknowledge that navigating therapists, insurance, special schools, among others, has been a different experience for me as a white middle-class woman with a stable job and benefits. My husband and I have choices regarding our daughter, whereas many people with disabled family members do not.

I worked in service positions in high school and college, but I regret some interactions I had with people different from me, which I know now were indicative of my unchecked privilege and lack of awareness of other cultures. Though I was a student teacher in a predominantly Black middle school in Mississippi, I knew very little about the cultures and backgrounds of the students I was working with. My classes at a private college were not diverse and did not prepare me for being a culturally competent or culturally humble teacher. From those experiences, it is no wonder I did not pursue teaching as a profession.

Returning to graduate school in the last few years, I found myself in two classes where I was in the minority, which is remarkable and humbling considering it is a predominantly white institution. It is invaluable to listen to the experiences of my peers and understand how different they were from mine. In a course on the history of higher education in the United States, we discussed racist and sexist policies and practices that still impact the ability of students of color to get advanced degrees. I took for granted that historically Black colleges and universities (HBCUs) were a uniquely southern phenomenon rooted in racism. After working at three southern universities and obtaining advanced degrees, I wondered, how did I not know more about higher education's deeply entrenched discriminatory practices?

For a long time, I have had the "luxury of obliviousness" afforded to those in the dominant group who do not have to be aware of their privilege (Johnson, 2017). As a straight white woman, I have always been accepted in the LIS field. There has never been an instance at a conference, committee, or in any professional setting where I was in the minority. I have not had to think about what it means to be me *and* to be a LIS professional.

My library reflects the racial makeup of the profession, with very few Black, Indigenous, and People of Color (BIPOC). We have only one Black tenure-track faculty member, which does not correspond with the makeup of the student body or the state's residents. I recently realized that during the last twenty years, only two BIPOC staff have worked in the special collections department, which I supervise.

I have not done enough to address these inequities. Direct recruitment of people from traditionally underrepresented or marginalized groups has been largely unsuccessful. However, as a library, we are continuing to identify and change our hiring practices to be more equitable and inclusive. Mostly by chance, I have been able to establish a graduate assistantship for BIPOC LIS students and help to acquire diverse collections, but there is much more work to be done.

By revealing my experiences and background and how both have impacted my perceptions of privilege, power, and cultural humility, I hope to challenge others to critically examine how their personal histories affect their understanding of the issues. I offer a strong disclaimer that I am still learning about cultural humility and its promise of a lifelong, more socially conscious journey. I am still determining how best to effect change in my role as a person with some degree of power in libraries. I have also realized that it can often feel like it's "never enough," but that can be framed as more of a rallying cry rather than a discouragement not to even try.

If you have power, consider ways you can effect positive change. Be willing to decenter your feelings and listen to others' experiences. Be vulnerable and approach situations with a mindset that allows you to examine your assumptions and acknowledge what you don't know or understand. Challenge yourself to reflect on the uncomfortable truths that historically and currently affect the LIS profession. Self-awareness, curiosity about others, and a willingness to learn are key to addressing issues of power and privilege as a culturally humble individual.

REFERENCES

ALA/ARL Building Cultural Proficiencies for Racial Equity Framework Task Force. (2022). *Cultural proficiencies for racial equity: A framework*. Chicago and Washington, DC: https://www.ala.org/advocacy/sites/ala.org.advocacy/files/content/diversity/ALA%20ARL%20Cultural%20Proficiencies%20for%20Racial%20Equity%20Framework.pdf

Brook, F., Ellenwood, D., & Lazzaro, A. E. (2016). In pursuit of antiracist social justice: Denaturalizing whiteness in the academic library. *Library Trends*, 64(2), 246–284.

Chugh, D. (2018, September 18). *Use your everyday privilege to help others*. Harvard Business Review. https://hbr.org/2018/09/use-your-everyday-privilege-to-help-others

Ebbitt, K. (2015). *Why it's important to think about privilege—and why it's hard*. Global Citizen. https://www.globalcitizen.org/en/content/why-its-important-to-think-about-privilege-and-why/

Galvan, A. (2015). *Soliciting performance, hiding bias: Whiteness and librarianship*. In the Library with the Lead Pipe. http://www.inthelibrarywiththeleadpipe.org/2015/soliciting-performance-hiding-bias-whiteness-and-librarianship/

Harris, L. (2019). *Diversity beyond lip service: A coaching guide for challenging bias*. Berrett-Koehler.

Johnson, A. G. (2017). The trouble we are in: Power, privilege, and difference. Maryville University. https://www.maryville.edu/wp-content/uploads/2017/05/Article-JohnsonTheTroubleWereIn-.pdf

Lawton, S. (2018). *Reflections on gender oppression and libraries*. Public Libraries Online. http://publiclibrariesonline.org/2018/03/reflections-on-gender-oppression-and-libraries/

McIntosh, P. (1989). White privilege: Unpacking the invisible knapsack. *Peace and Freedom*, 49(4), 10–12.

Norman, T., & Adelman, R. B. (2022). *Owning your privilege: Leaving guilt, shame, and blame behind*. Integrated Work [blog]. https://integratedwork.com/jedi/owning-your-privilege/

Sierpe, E. (2019). Confronting librarianship and its function in the structure of white supremacy and the ethno state. *Journal of Radical Librarianship*, 5, 84–102. https://www.journal.radicallibrarianship.org/index.php/journal/article/view/39

Tervalon, M., & Murray-Garcia, J. (1998). Cultural humility versus cultural competence: A critical distinction in defining physician training outcomes in multicultural education. *Journal of Health Care for the Poor and Underserved,* 9(2), 117–125. https://muse.jhu.edu/article/268076

U.S. Bureau of Labor Statistics (2020). *Household data annual averages: Employed persons by detailed occupation, sex, race, and Hispanic or Latino ethnicity.* https://www.bls.gov/cps/cpsaat11.pdf

12

Cultural Humility and Black Males in the Library

Conrad Pegues

"Cultural humility" is a term coined by Melanie Tervalon and Jann Murray-Garcia during their research on cultural competence in the medical field. Tervalon and Murray-Garcia found the usual term "cultural competence" to be insufficient in describing the physician-patient dynamic. "Cultural competence" could be subject to cultural stereotypes that help neither medical practitioner nor patient (Tervalon and Murray-Garcia, 1998, 119). Tervalon and Murray-Garcia coined "cultural humility" to frame the medical professional and the patient as colleagues in the healing process:

> Cultural humility incorporates a lifelong commitment to self-evaluation and critique, to redressing the power imbalances in the physician-patient dynamic, and to developing mutually beneficial and non-paternalistic partnerships with communities on behalf of individuals and defined populations. (1998, 123)

Cultural humility creates the best environment for the exchange of information to meet the needs of the patient. It also trains medical professionals to recognize that the patient is crucial to the healing process, as their history has informed their health choices and will inform their choices for healing.

In the library field, cultural humility is not only the expectation of giving good customer service but also the ability to be able to empathize with a patron and remove obstacles to accessing information. Unlike a physician's patient who presents with physical symptoms for diagnosis, the librarian may have no idea what issues a patron may have with information access. Cultural humility is "especially suited to library service, where power dynamics can be subtle and issues of identity complex" (Hurley, Kostelecky, & Townsend, 2019). The library professional provides empathetic service and an atmosphere where patrons are comfortable disclosing their needs without shame or judgment.

Historically in America, libraries have been contested spaces for Black Americans. In South Carolina beginning in 1740, it was illegal for Black people to read and write, a practice that other southern states adopted as well (Banks, 1996). Laws became even more stringent in 1831, after Nat Turner's revolt, out of fear that literate enslaved Blacks might revolt. Barriers to literature and library access remained strong throughout the Jim Crow era and segregation until the civil rights movement challenged racist ideologies and laws.

In addition, Black people's reading choices were often policed by white librarians, which Richard Wright highlights in his book *Black Boy*. Wright wanted to read H. L. Mencken's criticism of the segregated South, so to avoid suspicion, he borrowed a white coworker's library card to check it out (Wright, 1945). Some things have changed since that time, and some have not. Black bodies are still a point of contention in library spaces. As a Black man in the library field, I have seen firsthand how Black males move within public and academic libraries.

In this chapter I will particularly focus on the barriers for the bodies of Black male librarians and patrons in library spaces. I will relate my experiences of Black males in the library and the particular needs they bring in reaction to systemic racism in American culture. Based on my experiences as branch manager of the Hadley Park Library in the Nashville Public Library (NPL) system, I will give several instances where cultural humility became a bridge between myself and the particular needs that Black men brought through the library doors.

CULTURAL HUMILITY AND MENTAL HEALTH

Located in North Nashville, Tennessee, the Hadley Park Library opened its doors in 1952 to serve Black Nashville residents who were not welcome in other Nashville branches. North Nashville, a historically Black enclave intersected by Interstate 40, is presently grappling with issues of gentrification and rising crime rates, particularly around HBCUs Tennessee State University and Meharry Medical College. In addition to responding to the usual requests for books and videos, I also served patrons dealing with homelessness, substance abuse, and mental health challenges.

It was not unusual for me to interact with a patron engaged in a conversation with a person that nobody else could see. This could be frightening for some, but I had family members with similar issues, so it did not frighten me. Cultural humility allowed me to apply the same library rules for these patrons about noise levels as I would for any patrons, thereby keeping the conversations down so as not to disrupt other library patrons. This effort of adjusting to a person's ability to operate in the library enabled the patron to get what resources he or she needed—whether it be a book, video, or computer—or to use the facility to get out of the sweltering summer heat or freezing winter cold. Over time, I began to bring in mental health providers to talk to the community about mental health issues in the Black community and available services from local organizations. Attendance was not high. In the Black community, mental health challenges are often reduced to anecdotes for family and friends, not something to be discussed in public.

Drug and alcohol abuse were also issues within the area served by the Hadley Park Branch. The local drug dealers, whom I called street pharmacists, were stationed across the street from the library. Though I knew the patrons who bought drugs, whether marijuana or crack, judgment was not something they needed. The mindset of cultural humility allowed me to *see people* and not be disapproving. As I learned their personal stories over time, I was taken aback by how many of the street pharmacists' customers were older Black men and women using drugs to manage their anxiety, depression, and trauma.

I had an unspoken deal with one of the drug dealers through a piercing look and a nod of the head. On occasion he would come in to read a book and get out of the summer heat or winter cold, but no drug transactions were to take place in the Hadley Park Branch.

CULTURAL HUMILITY AND HOMOPHOBIA

Sometimes, cultural humility called for nuanced approaches to difficult patrons. I had a contentious relationship with one Black male patron, a crack addict, who did not like me because I was same-gender loving. It was not unusual for me to hear him whisper under breath, "sissy m*f*." I would turn, look at him, and smile to let him know I was nothing to play with. He hated me even more, but I never put him out of the library unless he fell asleep and started snoring loudly, which disrupted other patrons. His action of *whispering* "sissy" was an obvious admission of his own cowardice. Attitudinally, I was bigger than him, and having sized me up, he saw no victim. There was no need to add fuel to the fire by a loud exchange unless he spoke above a whisper. He did not have to like me, and I did not like him either, but he was not going to be disrespectful in my library. If his disrespect rose above a whisper, he would be suspended from the library for abusive language.

I eventually had to suspend him over other behavioral issues, but I do remember one of the last exchanges we had was fairly amusing. He was looking through the cushions of one of the chairs where he usually sat. We had a decent exchange: "You lose something?" I asked. He lied and said something I can't recall. I figured he had lost his crack rock, which he never found. I felt no need to lecture him about bringing drugs into the library. It was enough that he had lost his high, which left me giggling all the way to my office.

Cultural humility might look odd in a Black urban library surrounded by socioeconomic and health-care issues. But when confronted with this reality, you can either throw up your hands in frustration or try to eke out some livable solution for patrons to get what they need.

I had to practice cultural humility with a Black male patron I will call D.J., who would talk to the two female staff members but was visibly uncomfortable when I came to the public service desk. So I gave him a wide berth for his comfort. D.J. had been in jail for selling drugs, had just gotten out, and was looking for work. Having a felony drug conviction impacts legitimate employment, often leading to recidivism. Though I did not discuss my personal life with staff or patrons—"Oh, by the way, I'm same-gender loving, now back to library programming"—I know the streets enough to know when my sexuality might be an issue for another man. It is silly to me, but that does not mean Black men and women don't sense the difference or have issues around same-gender-loving Black men who don't fit a hypermasculine street image. I knew this before I came to Hadley Park Library.

I overheard D.J. lamenting his job search while he checked out children's books for his little girl and videos and intellectual reading, like Malcolm X, for himself. Being aware of programs like "Second Chance" in Memphis, Tennessee, where I am originally from, I looked for similar programs in Nashville. D.J. would come to the library often enough, and eventually I interjected myself into the conversation about jobs and told him to inquire about programs that gave convicted felons opportunities to work. Though I had his attention, I remember my clerk telling him under her breath, "He ain't gon' bother you." I smiled to myself as she gave him a comfortable buffer against his fears that if he let his guard down, he would somehow end up in my arms declaring he was my boo. I could have easily been offended, but I knew he had been in jail, was not a big guy for his build, and was easy on the eyes—all license for sexual assault by inmates with no moral center.

The cultural humility he needed was my not being offended at his homophobia. He needed information to escape the street-to-jail pipeline so he could be a physical presence in his daughter's life. Through cultural humility, I made D.J. aware that I had his best interests in mind even though the streets had trained him against me.

D.J. disappeared for a few months but eventually showed up again at the library. I did not recognize him as he had put more weight on his frame, so he made it his business to speak to me. He said he was "a'ight" (all right), but I had heard on the street that he had been in some trouble and had gone to stay with an out-of-town relative. In the process he had been "eating good" and was not in trouble with the law. Though we are not here to save anybody, it is the nature of cultural humility to help patrons where they are with the knowledge and services they need.

CULTURAL HUMILITY AND BOUNDARIES IN THE LIBRARY

In working with Black men coming into Hadley Park, cultural humility for me often meant interacting with people outside the realm of usual experience. On one occasion, a Black man came to the library needing to use a computer to get some family photos from Facebook and save them to a thumb drive. I showed him how to get on the computer and told him how to get the photos, then I stood back since I always try to give patrons their space. He had no idea how to work the mouse to get the photos, and when I explained it to him, he still did not understand.

I saw his hands clumsily managing the mouse. They were dark and calloused at the thumbs and forefingers. Having worked with people dealing with HIV/AIDS and crack addiction, I had seen similar calluses and crack pipe burns develop from constantly flicking a lighter to heat the glass pipe. He had parked his truck in the service drive in the back of the branch. In the truck bed were plastic bins, a large barbecue pit, and some other household items.

I had to put my hand on his to show him exactly how to get the photos by using the clipping tool if he could not download them. While steadily following my guidance, he began to show me more and more pictures, including some of him fishing with family members, different meals he had cooked when he had an apartment, his grown son and daughter, and a woman he called his girlfriend whom he had left because her children did not approve of their relationship. His brutalized hands told his story.

Cultural humility in this context was simply touching him and listening to him. I did not broach his trust to direct him to the nearest drug rehabilitation program at Meharry Hospital down the street. That was not my job. My immediate job was to show him how to use the computer to get his memories onto his thumb drive. Maybe the photos offered hope that he could get his life back. I felt neither contempt nor sympathy, only empathy.

Empathy is a crucial factor in exercising cultural humility in the library space, but there are more complex issues in an urban environment with historically inherited problems of racism. Like so many other Black people, I have debated at times whether or not to call the police.

There was an unkempt patron who had a habit of talking to invisible people who became belligerent with me because I would not let him spread out on the floor, make a tent, and take his shirt and shoes off. I asked him not to spread out his personal belongings across the floor or take his shirt off. But when, staring at me, he told his invisible people, "This librarian better leave me alone!" I had to call the police and suspend his entry into the library because of his threats to harm me.

He was not the first or the last patron to physically threaten me. One patron called the library to say I was a snitch, denoting betrayal to him by calling the police. I also had to be aware of Black boys whose behavior in the library I had to correct, as they might have gang affiliations that could put me and my staff in harm's way.

CULTURAL HUMILITY AND BLACK MANHOOD IN THE LIBRARY

Cultural humility is not about librarians putting themselves in harm's way. It is about providing the best services possible for patrons, and sometimes that means contacting the police to defuse dangerous situations. What cultural humility can offer in these potentially menacing situations is to err on the side of caution and the safety of library staff and patrons.

To give some semblance of safety to the library staff and patrons, I requested and received a part-time security officer. A security guard can be a great help, especially if the person understands the community where he or she is assigned. Since I had not made enough police reports to warrant a permanent guard, I could not always get one. Additionally, I was questioned by the white male director of branch services whether I was "in charge" of my branch. It was assumed that I did not need a guard like some of the branches that had white managers in neighborhoods without Hadley Park's problems. The presumption by the director was that as a big Black man, I should be able to handle criminal elements and threatening behaviors due to a natural affinity for dealing with drugs, drug dealers, alcoholism, mental health issues, and prostitution. Consequently, I interpreted and embraced all of this as questioning my manhood.

Where cultural humility should have come into play is understanding the stereotypical notions of putting a Black man in a "problem branch" located in a predominantly Black neighborhood, which for the NPL system includes Bordeaux, Edgehill, Looby, and Pruitt. As a Black, same-gender-loving male, I was a three-for-one diversity hire. Having an MLIS from Kent State was gravy.

CULTURAL HUMILITY AND LIBRARY ADMINISTRATION

Cultural humility operates by making colleagues and patrons see one another as human beings who live in systems of inequality that require active evaluation of policies that limit full access to libraries. (Cooke, 2017; Tervalon & Garcia, 1998). This action has to start from the top with library administration, who must set the tone for providing a culturally humble environment. To assume that Black people are intimate with dysfunction and trauma, rendering them invulnerable to the threat of violence without complaint, is rooted in racism.

For this particular narrative, library administration has much work to do in learning to practice cultural humility, as it must have a viable and compassionate support system to be fully operational. A start would be to investigate and explore various strategies, including providing training focused on diversity, equity, inclusion, and belonging; fostering communication through crucial conversations; and implementing a plan to put strategies into action.

To practice cultural humility in this library space will require contacts and library programming in health and mental health, social justice and services, and any other relevant topics that may help get information and services to the people who need them. The practice of cultural humility can profoundly affect how we create services and meet the needs of all those concerned. In the library field and the communities libraries serve, cultural humility is only as strong as those committed to its philosophy.

CONCLUSION

After almost three years of wrestling with the issues of Hadley Park Branch and my physician wanting to put me on antianxiety meds, I requested to be moved. The white female librarian who managed Hadley Park before me only lasted a few months before the neighborhood drama became too overwhelming. Subsequently, she was moved to a bigger branch in an area with less crime and given a pay increase and security guards. As for me, my feelings were downplayed by the branch manager of library services, and ultimately I was not moved. So, what is the moral of this story?

Eventually I left the Nashville Public Library system for both mental and physical health issues.

In the library field, cultural humility is about compassion. It can have a profound effect on how we meet the needs of patrons, but that compassion must include care and concern for the librarians who work every day to meet those needs.

REFERENCES

Banks, W. M. (1996). *Black intellectuals: Race and responsibility in American life*. W. W. Norton.

Cooke, N. (2017). *Information services to diverse populations: Developing culturally competent library professionals*. Libraries Limited.

Hurley, D. A., Kostelecky, S., & Townsend, L. (2019). Cultural humility in libraries. *Reference Services Review, 47*(4), 544–555.

Johnson, K., Quest, T., & Curseen, K. (2020). Will you hear me? Have you heard me? Do you see me? Adding cultural humility to resource allocation and priority setting discussions in the care of African American patients with COVID-19. *Journal of Pain and Symptom Management, 60*(5), e11–e14. https://www.sciencedirect.com/science/article/abs/pii/S0885392420307235?via%3Dihub

Tervalon, M., & Murray-Garcia, J. (1998). Cultural humility versus cultural competence: A critical distinction in defining physician training outcomes in multicultural education. *Journal of Health Care for the Poor and Underserved,* 9(2), 117–125.

Wright, Richard. (1945). *Black boy.* Harper Perennial.

13

Beyond the Rainbow

INTEGRATING CULTURAL HUMILITY INTO LGBTQIA+ HEALTH INCLUSION INITIATIVES

Jane Morgan-Daniel, David G. Keddle, Jacqueline Leskovec, Brenda M. Linares, Hannah M. Schilperoort, Meredith Solomon, Brandi Tuttle, and Emily Vardell

This chapter discusses how cultural humility has shaped the professional identities and advocacy journeys of eight librarians from academic, clinical, and hospital settings, all of whom identify as LGBTQIA+ (lesbian, gay, bisexual, transgender, queer or questioning, intersex, asexual, and plus for additional identities not currently represented in the acronym). Health sciences librarians have long advocated for the LGBTQIA+ community. Through activism and the centering of diversity, equity, and inclusion (DEI) in the profession, librarians have worked to eliminate health and health information disparities faced by these populations (Perry, 2020; Morris & Hawkins, 2016). This work has taken many forms, including outreach to health consumers, practitioners, and students; community health promotion; building more inclusive collections and pathfinders to improve information availability and accessibility; creating database search strategies encompassing LGBTQIA+ populations and issues; collaborating with health professions to incorporate LGBTQIA+ perspectives into curricula; and developing and promoting training for library employees on strategies to better meet the needs of LGBTQIA+ patrons through reference interactions, creating safe and affirming spaces, and using inclusive language (Hawkins et al., 2017; Morris & Roberto, 2016; Stevens et al., 2019; Vera, Wagner, & Kitzie, 2020).

As noted in the literature, LGBTQIA+ advocacy is certainly challenging as it involves working with the ever-present backdrop of issues such as censorship, marginalizing organizational policies and procedures, and experiences of discrimination among patrons and library employees. This work is often done alongside those who incorrectly assume that there are no specific health needs of LGBTQIA+ populations (Greenblatt, 2014; Hawkins et al., 2017; Perry, 2020). LGBTQIA+ health librarianship is an emerging field, and incorporating cultural humility into this work is essential. In doing so, we have the potential to meet people where they are while helping them to see that all information professionals have a role in ensuring that the needs of the LGBTQIA+ community are met equitably.

All authors are members of the Medical Library Association (MLA) LGBTQIA+ Caucus and have previously collaborated to present immersion sessions on LGBTQIA+ inclusion practices and initiatives in health sciences libraries at the MLA 2020 and 2021 annual conferences. In this chapter, the authors describe how their own identities have motivated their involvement in LGBTQIA+ inclusion initiatives, how they strive to infuse cultural humility into the work they do, and the challenges they have faced in their current institutions. We use the acronym LGBTQIA+, the most common acronym currently used within the LGBTQIA+ community today, and the acronym used in the latest iteration of the title of the MLA LGBTQIA+ Caucus. As with all language use, LGBTQIA+ terms are constantly evolving and have changed over time as the LGBTQIA+ community strives to become more inclusive to the multiplicity of voices and identities within our community.

POSITIONALITY STATEMENT

The authors of this chapter represent various personal backgrounds, including diversity of race and ethnicity, gender, sexual orientation, family structure, socioeconomic level, age, veteran status, and professional role. They have experience serving on DEI committees within professional associations and at their institutions. They do not, however, purport to represent all communities within the umbrella of DEI efforts as they can only speak to their own experiences and backgrounds. For example, this group of authors is composed entirely of cisgender individuals and therefore cannot speak to the experiences of transgender individuals. Our stories and experiences are shared through the lens of cultural humility, which can be defined as "a lifelong process and commitment to self-evaluation, learning, reflection, and understanding other cultures" (Applegate, 2018). Cultural humility in relation to the LGBTQIA+ community involves the use of proper pronouns, gender-inclusive language, and the decentering of cisnormativity and heteronormativity. The discussions laid out in this chapter invite all to the table so more perspectives can be included.

David Keddle

For the past sixteen years, my library has provided LGBTQIA+ information in a hospital setting. Since 2005, the library has maintained a consumer health collection, including many books on all aspects of LGBTQIA+ health information. When I accepted the position of medical library services director, Kaiser Permanente Woodland Hills Medical Center, California, I developed this collection for all staff and patients, as the library prides itself on cultural humility and being open and affirming to all who visit. On a personal note, being older when I came out and coming from a very conservative town, it was a huge struggle for me.

In developing inclusive library services, I aimed to make it easier for the LGBTQIA+ population to have a place to go for information where they would not feel threatened in any way. I designated my office as a safe space for all, using the Human Rights Campaign's equality sign on the door for visibility, so that any individuals who felt they needed a place to visit to discuss LGBTQIA+ topics could do so in a confidential space. I found that many staff wanted to talk about how best to support LGBTQIA+ family, friends, and coworkers, both in terms of health-care needs and also when families were going through the coming-out process. The library has become the go-to place for all potentially culturally sensitive questions. Patron requests are kept totally confidential as we are a safe place environment, and it is Kaiser Permanente policy to keep patrons' communications private.

In order to better address the needs of LGBTQIA+ employees, I helped develop a local chapter of Kaiser Permanente (KP) Pride for which I'm currently the president. As part of this, KP Pride holds meetings and provides programming to enhance understanding of the needs of LGBTQIA+ employees. Annually, we host a multicultural day to educate all employees on the multiple cultures of Woodland Hills staff. In 2014, the homeless navigator at the medical center visited my office to talk about challenges that local homeless LGBTQIA+ people were experiencing when trying to use the Los Angeles community center. Frontline staff were not open to helping LGBTQIA+ youth access the care that they needed. Accordingly, Woodland Hills KP Pride developed a summit to facilitate a better understanding of the issues faced by LGBTQIA+ homeless youth in the San Fernando Valley. This was originally an all-day event held at the Woodland Hills Medical Center, with staff invited from many community centers in the West Hollywood area. The summit was so well received that it ran for the next five years, with the last event being held at a local hotel in Woodland Hills due to the large number of staff attending.

Jacqueline Leskovec

Since studying library science in the last millennium, I have unconsciously followed a pattern of integrating sexual and gender minority perspectives into my day-to-day work. Currently, as the network coordinator for Region 6 of the Network of the National Library of Medicine (NNLM), I have made LGBTQIA+ health information a priority, incorporating cultural humility even while being a member of the community.

I first became involved in LGBTQIA+ advocacy within librarianship as a student in a course titled "Academic Libraries." I put together a short training on how to access what we now call LGBTQIA+ health information. Essential to that session was the reference interview and how to provide a supportive environment for patrons who might consider this a sensitive topic. In the 1990s, being out and open as a member of the community was less acceptable than it is today. Even the website for MLA's Lesbian, Gay, Bisexual and Transgendered (sic) Health Science Librarians Special Interest Group (SIG), the precursor to the current LGBTQIA+ Caucus, provided the following caveat at the time:

> This SIG's membership is not limited to gay persons, but rather is open to any member of MLA who supports anti-discrimination and is pro-human rights. We welcome you! However, this page is a partial list of active SIG members. With discrimination and prejudice still present in our society, it is not possible for some individuals to be on such a roster for a variety of professional and personal reasons. It is our hope that in the future, such concerns will be irrelevant. Until that time, this list will likely not be complete.
>
> (Lesbian, Gay, Bisexual and Transgendered Health Science Librarians Special Interest Group (SIG) of the Medical Library Association, n.d.)

Another similarly focused school assignment followed with the creation of an online pathfinder for lesbian health. Gough and Greenblatt's seminal work *Gay and Lesbian Library Service* (1990) was one of the few print resources available on the topic at that time.

As a professional librarian, I have continued this integrative approach. At the 2014 MLA Annual Conference in Chicago, I gave a presentation on "Lesbian, Gay, Bisexual, Transgender Privacy Issues" during a program sponsored by the then Relevant Issues Section. Despite great strides being made on political and social levels (e.g., the repeal of "Don't Ask, Don't Tell" and the introduction of marriage equality bills), safeguarding sexual orientation or gender identity was still a priority.

A few decades later in my position as an NNLM coordinator, I have taken a more direct approach to improving LGBTQIA+ health information access by coauthoring NNLM MLA CE classes such as "Beyond the Binary: Health Resources for Sexual and Gender Minorities," inviting webinar speakers for LGBTQIA+ Pride Month, and working with others in the caucus to present at national conferences, such as MLA. I also work with MLA colleagues to update sexual and gender minorities' health information resources on the caucus website. I continue to make LGBTQIA+ health information access essential to my work, such as integrating the needs of sexual and gender minorities in times of COVID-19, disasters, and emergency preparedness. In the quest to maintain cultural humility, health information outreach to LGBTQIA+ populations does not require reinventing the wheel. Avail yourself of quality training to find and assess health information for these populations. Maintain awareness of their cultural position and health priorities. Listen to the myriad voices in this chapter and ask yourself, "How can I integrate the LGBTQIA+ perspective in my work?"

Brenda Linares

As a Latina, immigrant, and gay woman, I have had many conversations about diversity—these have always been a part of my life. There is so much intersectionality in who I am and what I do as a librarian. Teaching the importance of DEI and LGBTQIA+ and bringing it into conversations has always been important to me. As someone who has experienced microaggressions in many instances and who feels that people make judgments about me before getting to know me, I believe it is essential to use teachable moments to discuss the importance of DEI and LGBTQIA+ issues. Cultural humility is a critical aspect that we should never forget because we learn from one another. No one can be an expert when it comes to DEI, because each person has his or her own story and experience, and we all need to keep an open mind about who people are.

Before taking on my current role as associate dean of library services, University of Missouri–Kansas City (UMKC) University Libraries, I was at the University of Kansas Medical Center (KUMC) for four and a half years. I saw the campus there become more inclusive and more open to conversations about DEI and LGBTQIA+ issues. I experienced a lot of positive changes, but when I say that, it does not mean that it was bad before. It means I saw a move forward in helping the LGBTQIA+ community to be seen and to create a safe space for us to meet and discuss issues that were important to us.

For example, in the summer of 2019, the DEI office organized a small pride picnic cookout for Pride Month. A few of us attended and discussed that it would be great to have a more organized group to gather and support LGBTQIA+ issues. Then in 2020, we had a bigger and more inclusive celebration during Pride Month. Because I had been at the picnic the year before and was also part of the campus DEI Cabinet, I volunteered to help. Due to COVID-19, all these events took place virtually. Our programming followed the same logistics and events as heritage month celebrations. We organized a virtual Coffee Break where people participated in casual morning chat and networking. We also organized a Community Conversations event around the word "queer" and how the meaning of this word has changed through the years. This stimulated a great open discussion between the younger and older members of the LGBTQIA+ community, where we were all amenable to learning from one another. To continue the celebration, biographical posters featured personal stories of LGBTQIA+ campus members. These programs were a success and well attended, and in 2021 we included them along with a research day to showcase research done by LGBTQIA+ members and research related to LGBTQIA+ topics.

Since we were organizing these events and getting together, we decided to create PRISM, KUMC's LGBTQIA+ affinity group, to bring about issues that were important to students, staff, and faculty. Our work was informed by our vision, "a campus where all sexual orientations, gender identities, and gender expressions are accepted and affirmed," and our purpose, "to advocate for LGBTQ+ individuals and allies through the support of campus-wide activities and goals to enhance visibility, foster professionalism, and empower conversations that inspire systemic change and challenge discrimination within the KUMC community." The group was very successful in obtaining funding from KUMC during its first year to purchase pronoun buttons for work badges at both the medical campus and hospital. PRISM has continued its work and commitment to creating an inclusive campus.

Jane Morgan-Daniel

I currently serve as community engagement and health literacy liaison librarian, University of Florida Health Science Center Libraries. As previous lead and current member of the DEI Team at my library, I have codeveloped programming, space, and resource-related initiatives to enhance inclusivity and amplify the voices of LGBTQIA+ patrons and employees. My professional journey has most certainly been shaped by my identity as a bisexual, white, British-American, cisgender woman. I am continually and intentionally learning about other people's perspectives and experiences while striving to recognize my own biases. I try to integrate cultural humility into all aspects of my position. I collaborate with community-based groups as well as health professions departments, and much of my work relates to the health information needs of underserved and underrepresented groups.

So far, I feel the most impactful initiative conducted at my library to improve inclusivity for our LGBTQIA+ communities was a panel created and hosted by the DEI Team in 2019 and 2021 called "Honoring LGBTQIA+ Health Stories." The panel formed part of the College of Medicine's Celebration of Diversity Week. Its purpose was to educate future health providers on the health needs of LGBTQIA+ patients by providing an opportunity for panelists, who identified as LGBTQIA+ themselves, to share their experiences as healthcare providers. Questions for the panelists included:

- What positive or negative health-care experiences do you feel comfortable sharing?

- How could health-care providers enhance service provision for those identifying as LGBTQIA+?
- How could educators within the medical and health professions improve their students' understanding of the health needs of LGBTQIA+ communities?

Panel attendance surpassed our expectations, with over one hundred in-person attendees in 2019 and seventy-two for the virtual version in 2021. Feedback has been overwhelmingly positive—attendees felt extremely engaged by the panelists' descriptions of their personal journeys, with faculty asking for the recordings to share in future classes. The most significant challenge was recruiting panelists with intersecting identities to encompass different facets of LGBTQIA+ experiences. This is an issue that we will continue working on for the 2022 iteration of the panel, which is likely to shift focus to include the voices of community members as well as health professionals.

Other library efforts have included enhancing employees' ally skills through purchasing access to the Foundational Safe Zone training curriculum. The DEI Team has also encouraged employees to become more aware of implicit biases related to sexuality, gender identity, and gender expression by undertaking optional anonymous tests through Project Implicit. For our digital and physical library spaces, we have added pride flags on our plasma screens to welcome visitors. We publicize LGBTQIA+ collections through our website, have advocated for all gender restrooms in the building, and have installed a lactation pod that's available for use by people of all gender identities.

Hannah Schilperoort

My identity as a queer woman and lesbian has definitely motivated my involvement in LGBTQIA+ DEI initiatives. However, any discrimination I have faced in my life as a result of my sexual orientation has always been mitigated by the privileges I have experienced as a middle-class white cisgender woman. For me, cultural humility means that even though I am part of the LGBTQIA+ community, it is important that I never speak for the entire community and that I recognize my own privileges and biases. As head of the Wilson Dental Library at the University of Southern California (USC), I strive to practice cultural humility in the work that I do by emphasizing the multiplicity of identities and intersectionality within the LGBTQIA+ community and the multiple forms of oppression experienced by members of the LGBTQIA+ community.

For example, I have created two interactive LGBTQIA+ tutorials with another USC librarian, Holly Thompson, to help health sciences faculty incorporate LGBTQIA+ cultural competency into the curriculum. The tutorials cover current topics and issues facing the LGBTQIA+ community within health care; strategies for creating a welcoming and inclusive clinical environment; social determinants of health, health disparities, and intersectionality within the

LGBTQIA+ community; and the nuances between cultural competency and cultural humility. We intentionally highlighted studies that show that trans people and people of color within the LGBTQIA+ community experience more health disparities and more discrimination in health care than their white cisgender counterparts. We wanted to emphasize that the LGBTQIA+ community is just as diverse in terms of race, ethnicity, language, culture, gender, sexual orientation, class, education, and other social characteristics as the larger population, and thus many members of the community experience multiple forms of discrimination.

Another challenge we faced when creating the tutorials was the difference between cultural competency and cultural humility. Competency implies that there are a set of standards that individuals can learn to become culturally competent in all situations and contexts, while cultural humility acknowledges that language and practices are contextual and constantly changing, and it involves a lifelong commitment to self-reflection and self-critique about one's own beliefs, biases, and assumptions (Yeager & Bauer-Wu, 2013). We prefer the term "cultural humility" because of its emphasis on self-reflection and discovery, but we used the term "cultural competency" in the title of one of the tutorials and multiple times throughout both tutorials because this is the most established term in health-care education, and we wanted faculty and students to recognize that the tutorials were directly addressing a concept in their curriculum. To help mitigate this, we included a discussion of the differences between cultural competency and cultural humility in the beginning of the first tutorial.

Meredith Solomon

I am the senior outreach officer at Countway Library of Medicine, which serves Harvard Medical School, Harvard School of Dental Medicine, and Harvard T. H. Chan School of Public Health. Identifying as a lesbian was the primary reason I became involved in LGBTQIA+ and DEI work. I have been lucky (mostly because of my white privilege) to not have been discriminated against due to my sexual orientation or skin color, even while working at Harvard. That being said, I am always seeking out and investigating new opportunities to serve and be a part of the change at my institution and within my library—be it systematically, departmentally, or individually.

Some of the initiatives I have been involved with include:

- working with faculty, staff, residents, and fellows by performing literature searches about integrating sexual and gender minority (SGM) case studies and providing examples to be inclusive for the entire medical school curriculum rather than a single SGM course;
- adding my name to the HMS OUTlist of colleagues that students, staff, and faculty can reach out to and connect with;

- creating a Diversity, Inclusion, Belonging (DIB) browsable collection with an electronic form for users to submit collection suggestions;
- hosting in-person and virtual events throughout the year on DEI topics including sexual and gender identity, ableism, and equity issues;
- creating an LGBTQIA+ LibGuide;
- highlighting topics during certain monthly observances;
- establishing a student outreach advisory group to ensure Countway is supporting our students as inclusively as we can.

It is through these endeavors that I practice cultural humility and lean in to learn from those with different lived experiences than I have had. This allows us all to grow and be the people we mean to be.

Brandi Tuttle

My journey of discovering and accepting my intersectionality has certainly been one of fits and starts. Growing up in a small Midwest town in extreme poverty while helping care for my disabled mother (who passed away while I was a teen) deeply rooted the conviction that I always needed to be a strong, self-sufficient individual. Vulnerabilities, identities, and needs were routinely ignored, suppressed, or repressed. My knowledge of and experience with cultural humility began in college during my studies in anthropology and sociology. After graduate school, I was a public librarian, volunteer zine librarian, and an adult literacy and ESL (English as a second language) tutor for a few years before moving to Duke, which offered many eye-opening experiences.

But my background, including five years of military experience, certainly enabled, or required (due to the U.S. policy of "Don't ask, don't tell" on military service by gay men, bisexuals, and lesbians) the denial of my many-faceted identities and clashed with what I was beginning to learn. Over the last decade or so, I have expanded the concept of my intersectionality to include identifying as a white, queer, cisgender woman who is also a mother, divorcée, Indigenous American, and veteran. It is through and because of these many lenses that I began to connect with students and faculty as an advocate, educator, and ally. Cultural humility has given me a framework to approach my work (and life) where I continue examining my own identities, biases, and beliefs in addition to learning more about those around me.

Having been a research and education librarian at Duke University Medical Center Library and Archives for over seventeen years now, I am excited to see many efforts dedicated to the LGBTQIA+ community. I decided to make DEI one of my professional goals, and to that end, I chaired our library's Diversity and Inclusion Committee to strengthen our internal library programming and education efforts. I also ran a book club for staff, advocated for gender-neutral bathrooms and signage in the library, pulled together a group to provide feedback on our current hiring practices, provided staff with DEI-related information and events, and secured sessions for all staff on issues related to LGBTQIA+ and intersectionality, which were conducted by a diversity trainer over the summer of 2020. As part of the Physician Assistant Program's Curriculum Committee, I joined work groups on Women's Health and Sexuality where we incorporated more LGBTQIA+ health topics and information throughout the didactic year. These initiatives also dovetailed with a hard look at cases and vignettes presented with the goal to diversify the cases.

During this time, I was invited to join the Duke Department of Family Medicine and Community Health's LGBTQIA+ Community Advisory Board for Durham and their Diversity and Inclusion Committee. These collaborations have allowed me to engage with both the Duke and Durham communities as a librarian and an LGBTQIA+ community member. One challenge with the Community Advisory Board is sustaining community involvement and participation in our evening meetings, especially once the pandemic hit and many of our plans (e.g., Pride parade info booth) were canceled. The Duke Health presence is strong as researchers are excited to engage with the LGBTQIA+ community and discuss (or proudly announce) new initiatives, such as finally getting SOGIE (sexual orientations, gender identities and expressions) questions in the electronic health record. I have been trying to help the board work more efficiently by setting up a listserv and starting a LibGuide, but neither has found traction yet since the board doesn't have a staff member who is able to dedicate enough time. Sometimes forward progress seems small, but when I have a student come to me because they feel safer or they finally feel included, I am reminded of the importance of this work even when it feels like a tiny step.

Emily Vardell

I am currently an assistant professor in the School of Library and Information Management at Emporia State University (ESU). My experiences as a gay woman have certainly informed my approach to DEI work, as well as the fact that I am both the daughter of an immigrant and the wife of an immigrant. I see the intersectionalities of diversity work and recognize that there are needs that are unique to specific communities. I also recognize that diversity work has the potential to cut across barriers and create lasting change.

I seek out opportunities to serve and help enact change in my institution. One specific example of how this has occurred grew out of my service in our University Diversity and Inclusion Alliance. I was tasked along with another faculty member to complete our university's response to the Campus Pride Index, "the premier LGBTQ national benchmarking tool for colleges and universities to create safer, more inclusive campus communities" (https://www.campusprideindex.org/). One of the needs that was identified through this work was the establishment of an LGBTQIA+ Advisory Council for faculty and staff. Though the council is still in its early stages, we have already addressed changes needed in university policy, helped improve campus IT systems (e.g., updating names and gender information), and increased the visibility of LGBTQIA+ work within our campus.

We are currently at work creating an LGBTQIA+ Archive of ESU activists and activism through the years. While some may think a small regional university in Kansas may not have a rich history of LGBTQIA+ activism, our work has shown that we, in fact, do have stories to tell (however difficult it may be to track down the information and find help with processing the materials!). The archive will include oral histories as well as documentation of the different initiatives that have been undertaken by Emporia students, alums, faculty, and staff. Prioritizing regular meetings and identifying partners from across the campus (including the Office of Diversity and interested alumni) has helped our group address the challenges of a lack of funding and staff time devoted to this project.

CONCLUSION

This chapter provides examples of integrating cultural humility and LGBTQIA+ advocacy work into practice within a variety of library settings at different organizational levels, including academic, clinical, and hospital. As members of the LGBTQIA+ community, the authors present a wide range of strategies for enhancing the DEI environment for LGBTQIA+ library patrons, health providers, and patients in relation to library programming, policies, training, instruction, services, space, collection development, and community engagement. Challenges to implementing inclusive and equitable initiatives include micro/macroaggressions, privacy and safety issues with disclosing identities, lack of funding and employee time, and the ability to sustain change through encouraging continual community involvement and participation.

In addition, the authors discuss the importance of recognizing intersectionality while also being aware that each community has unique information needs. These information needs are exemplified when considering the LGBTQIA+ community, who collectively face common health disparities as a group while at the same time confronting specific health needs within individualized communities under the LGBTQIA+ umbrella. LGBTQIA+ health librarianship is an emerging field, and we invite all information professionals to contribute to the ongoing work of decentering cisnormativity and heteronormativity, so that the health information needs of the LGBTQIA+ community can be equitably met.

REFERENCES

Applegate, J. (2018). Cultural humility and LGBTQ communities in the healthcare environment. *Leadership in Healthcare and Public Health*. Ohio State University Pressbooks.

Gough, C., & Greenblatt, E. (1990). *Gay and lesbian library service*. McFarland.

Greenblatt, E. (2011). *Serving LGBTIQ library and archives users: Essays on outreach, service, collections and access*. McFarland.

Hawkins, B. W., Morris, M., Nguyen, T., Siegel, J., & Vardell, E. (2017). Advancing the conversation: Next steps for lesbian, gay, bisexual, trans, and queer (LGBTQ) health sciences librarianship. *Journal of the Medical Library Association, 105*(4), 316–327. https://doi.org/10.5195/jmla.2017.206

Lesbian, Gay, Bisexual and Transgendered Health Science Librarians Special Interest Group (SIG) of the Medical Library Association. (n.d.). *Members*. Last updated July 7, 2006. https://web.archive.org/web/20060709045809/http://lgbt.mlanet.org/members.html

Morris, M., & Hawkins, B. W. (2016). Towards a new specialization in health librarianship: LGBTQ health. *Journal of the Canadian Health Libraries Association, 37*(1), 20–23. https://doi.org/10.5596/c16-007

Morris, M., & Roberto, K. R. (2016). Information-seeking behaviour and information needs of LGBTQ health professionals: A follow-up study. *Health Information and Libraries Journal, 33*(3), 204–221. https://doi.org/10.1111/hir.12139

Perry, G. J. (2020). The activist health sciences librarian. *Journal of the Medical Library Association, 108*(1), 5–16. https://doi.org/10.5195/jmla.2020.859

Stevens, G. A., Morris, M., Nguyen, T., & Vardell, E. (2019). Health sciences librarians in the field: Pioneers for LGBTQ+ health. In B. Mehra (ed.), *Advances in Librarianship* (pp. 65–87). Emerald Publishing Limited.

Vera, A. N., Wagner, T. L., & Kitzie, V. L. (2020). "When it's time to come together, we come together": Reconceptualizing theories of self-efficacy for health information practices within LGBTQIA+ communities. In B. S. Jean (ed.), *Advances in Librarianship* (pp. 263–282). Emerald Publishing Limited.

Yeager, K. A., & Bauer-Wu, S. (2013). Cultural humility: Essential foundation for clinical researchers. *Applied Nursing Research, 26*(4), 251–256. https://doi.org/10.1016/j.apnr.2013.06.008

14

Trans Inclusivity

Travis L. Wagner

Cultural knowledge around transgender and nonbinary (T/GNB) identities, though increasing, remains limited due to cisnormative biases. Cisnormativity is the assumption that a person's gender identity matches their sex assigned at birth (i.e., cisgender) and, as a result, social spaces and systems center cisgender individuals. Spaces like public bathrooms are focal points for T/GNB individuals challenging cisnormativity. Libraries by design perpetuate cisnormativity (Barriage et al., 2021). Cisnormativity's persistence comes in the wake of detailed, practitioner-oriented texts on T/GNB inclusion applied across LIS (Krueger, 2019). Despite inclusive guidelines, trans-exclusionary actions persist against T/GNB patrons and practitioners. From my experience as a nonbinary person, this can be observed in instances where library conferences go to great lengths to provide gender-neutral bathrooms and pronoun pins yet fail to establish systems for reporting transphobic behavior within such spaces. Heath Fogg Davis (2018) suggests that this is an issue of policy lagging behind cultural shifts.

This chapter provides suggestions for navigating cultural humility; however, I want to offer two prefacing points. First, I can only speak from my personal vantage point of T/GNB identity. I am an AMAB (assigned male at birth) genderqueer person, an identity that differs from other identities encompassed by the T/GNB umbrella (i.e., trans, agender). I am also white, able-bodied, and hold a doctoral degree. These things afford me structural privileges within white supremacist and capitalist constructs. Accordingly, the suggestions that follow represent best practices but should not be regarded as the *only* practices available.

PRACTICE 1: MOVING BEYOND TRANS KNOWLEDGE TO INCLUSIVE HUMILITY

I recall attending a librarianship conference a few years back when I joined both initiatives related to LGBTQIA+ issues and groups working on building gender studies collections within academic libraries. I was committed to assuring that each was doing its part to promote T/GNB inclusivity, but unfortunately I was disappointed on both counts. During a discussion at my table, I recall raising the issue of the need for more visible support for trans patrons in southern libraries. Though folks seemed to acknowledge that this was a problem, they noted that their larger metropolitan libraries had already "figured out" this problem. Later that day, I attended a gender studies resources group session with another nonbinary colleague. Unsurprisingly, we were the only ones to share our pronouns in a room full of academic librarians tasked with curating materials for gender studies at their institutions. When asked by the committee chairs what we thought "our community" needed, we advocated for centering resources on being a T/GNB person. We noted that this could be a really inclusive practice considering that many academics lacked such information. The individuals in the room sat in silence before shifting the conversation back to their favorite women's history.

The institutional representatives I engaged with failed to understand how T/GNB identities operate as a spectrum rather than fixed identities. The LGBTQIA+ advocacy group presumed issues of transgender identity to be "solved" because they occupied progressive spaces that supported T/GNB individuals. The second anecdote highlights gender and knowledge essentialism. The committee's isolated view on informational resources favored authoritative, institutional information, which may not be relevant or inclusive for T/GNB communities. Essentializing information coincided with the implication that the concepts of women and gender were inherently cisgender. No mention was made of how women's studies needed to encompass broader concerns of femme identities, non-cisgender versions of masculinity, and other gender nonbinary identities. While there was understanding of the need for gender-inclusive practice, the cultural practice of inclusivity failed to expand the concepts of cisnormative womanhood. When practicing cultural humility with regards to inclusivity, it is equally important that practitioners simultaneously understand the ongoing work within T/GNB communities.

PRACTICE 2: IDENTIFYING STRUCTURAL FAILURES BEFORE T/GNB INDIVIDUALS DO

T/GNB individuals want to utilize libraries for more than just access to gender-neutral bathrooms (though this is important). I once had a student in a gender studies course who had recently come out as trans. During a research meeting he expressed frustrations in not finding anything related to transgender history.

I inquired quite candidly if he had tried any outdated terms in his search for describing T/GNB persons. Understandably he said no, assuming the library would avoid utilizing outdated terms. After incorporating one of the terms, I showed him my findings, and he was taken aback. Though the databases certainly had information to support his needs, the lack of community-affirming language was disappointing. I encouraged him to seek out materials, but he seemed less inclined to enter the library. Anticipating his apprehension of navigating a new space, I offered to go with him to the stacks. Together, we found multiple rows of transgender studies, gender nonbinary memoirs, and queer histories. As we explored, his concerns evaporated, and he found *himself* in the library. Regardless of one's gender, libraries can be incomprehensible. Though it may not be feasible to spend time and labor personally directing each user to a collection, cultural humility is about offering affect-driven support. While it is never appropriate to ask patrons their gender identity, their interest in finding T/GNB materials reveals a lot. Seeking out T/GNB memoirs, for instance, might suggest a desire to connect with the T/GNB community. Without noting the potential T/GNB identity, one could point to T/GNB communal resources rather than academic research about T/GNB populations.

Archie Crowley and I (2020) call attention to the troubling ways that even the most gender-forward academic libraries tend not to provide resource-based support for T/GNB individuals. Even academic institutions with visible support to T/GNB individuals engage in exclusionary actions, such as linking out to electronic databases which persistently deadname and misgender openly T/GNB authors. Our study suggests that even culturally competent practitioners overlook cisnormativity. A practitioner hoping to address the systemic failures faced by T/GNB patrons might consider some of the following actionable items as a way to be more inclusive:

- Practice bibliographic quality control measures for records. Check for proper pronoun usage and naming preferences throughout the records.
- Provide contextual guidance and even content warnings for shelving choices. If outdated terms are still in your catalog records or books are shelved in a certain way, be prepared to explain why.
- Signal a willingness to get feedback for gender-inclusive practices. While you might already have a feedback form, consider incorporating API elements or including signage to invite patrons to share their comments.

PRACTICE 3: MOVING CULTURAL SUPPORT TO POLICIES OF SUPPORT

I recall working with another researcher on a project focused on LGBTQIA+ health information practices that involved us interviewing queer community leaders. Given our relationship to libraries, we often suggested participants meet us at public libraries since they tended to be supportive spaces for

LGBTQIA+ individuals. One library expressed written support for doing our research in their library. Upon arrival, we were greeted by a welcoming staff who showed us to a room where we would be conducting the interview. When our participants showed up and began the interview, they seemed surprised that we were able to secure an interview space as they had previously experienced hostility from staff at this same library. While they were confused by this contradiction, we assured the participants that we had permission to be there. Nonetheless, thirty minutes into the interview, a completely different set of staff members began hovering around our designated space and staring. I stepped out of the room and asked if there were issues and was told we did not have permission to be in the space. I assured the staff member we did have permission and even showed them the email of support we had received. This did help to deter the problem in the moment, but upon returning to the interview, one of the participants stated, "I told you we have to deal with this [expletive] here all the time."

Though it would be easy to just write off this interaction as miscommunication, considering that all the participants were queer, the encounter read as anti-queer and confrontational. It also served as a reminder to myself and my colleague that support for our work was hardly universal. Months later this same library was embroiled in a battle over their funding due to their hosting a Drag Queen Story Time. Since the library did not have a rigid policy in place for supporting LGBTQIA+ communities, queer inclusion became an issue subject to regulation.

Enacting policy that is affirmative of T/GNB identity can lead to backlash. Though policies can have a significant impact on the funding and support of libraries, this visibility can negatively impact progress for T/GNB communities. Misdirected attempts at T/GNB support can lead to an intensification of legal and social barriers. Inclusive policymaking means avoiding ambiguity around the presence of and support for T/GNB persons (Davis, 2018). Without explicit policies, employees may circumvent aiding T/GNB communities. Libraries can appeal to national laws on gender equity, but if a state is antagonistic to T/GNB populations, making such appeals visible can lead to an entrenchment of anti-T/GNB sentiment. Navigation of banned books continues to be fruitful for inspiration on policy-driven librarian practices. Book-banning policies value preparing for backlash and producing clear, rooted, and established practices regarding intellectual freedom and inclusivity with a well-established paper trail (Austin, 2019). While each library's policy will undoubtedly look different, some elements worth considering include:

- Explicitly state that gender discrimination includes all gender identities. If this means listing out some T/GNB identities, so be it.
- Justify policies for obtaining services that require the use of government-issued IDs, but avoid relying on gender markers for any reason.
- Include explicit discussions around gender diversity in employee onboarding.

One tangible way to become invested in cultural humility as it relates to T/GNB populations is to shift away from viewing your library as the exclusive site of information access. Practitioners should prioritize support of the organization, preservation, and sustainability of communal resources. The role of a librarian here is not to be a provider of information but, if called upon, a curator of resources. Librarians who are passionate about helping T/GNB communities from a vantage point of cisgender identity could provide basic content-management tools and documentation schemas to help community members curate their already rich resources. It is important that this work not be about saving a community, as this could perpetuate deficit frameworks that falsely presume T/GNB persons as information illiterate (Gibson & Martin, 2019). As noted by others, listening to the needs of T/GNB communities often goes a lot farther than attempting to identify needs through cursory glances.

IMAGINING TRANS-INCLUSIVE CULTURAL HUMILITY

Librarians hoping to engage in cultural humility with T/GNB individuals and their communities might consider following an iterative auditing of their practices. Many community members will offer advice as a labor of love, but such work overlooks the economic inequities disproportionately impacting T/GNB populations. Sharing information openly and making it accessible is an essential part of this cultural humility work. Such an ecosystem of sharing enables many librarians to work through the unique challenges of T/GNB inclusivity. As a librarian you can start this work by committing to expanding your inclusive practices beyond the traditional realms of the stacks and reference desk.

REFERENCES

Austin, J. (2019). Representative library collections as a response to the institutional oppression of LGBTQ youth of color. *The International Journal of Information, Diversity, & Inclusion (IJIDI)*, 3(1).

Barriage, S. C., Kitzie, V., Floegel, D., & Oltmann, S. M. (2021). Drag queen storytimes: Public library staff perceptions and experiences. *Children and Libraries*, 19(2), 14–22.

Davis, H. F. (2018). *Beyond trans: Does gender matter?* NYU Press.

Gibson, A. N., & Martin III, J.D. (2019). Re-situating information poverty: Information marginalization and parents of individuals with disabilities. *Journal of the Association of Information Science and Technology*, 70(5), 476–487.

Krueger, S. G. (2019). *Supporting trans people in libraries*. Libraries Unlimited.

Wagner, T. L., & Crowley, A. (2020). Why are bathrooms inclusive if the stacks exclude? Systemic exclusion of trans and gender nonconforming persons in post-Trump academic librarianship. *Reference Services Review*, 48(1), 159–181.

15

Refugee Health

Kunga Denzongpa

Of the global population, eighty-six million are displaced persons (UNHCR, 2019), and this number will only grow as globalization expands over time. Refugees are eligible for resettlement to any country that accepts their residence but they are unable to seek residence in their country of origin. Resettlement sometimes can be temporary or permanent depending on the resettling country's policies. For example, the United States has permanently accepted Bhutanese refugees making them eligible to gain residency and eventually citizenship in the United States. Bhutanese refugees, however, are unable to seek residence in Bhutan, the country that forcibly displaced them from their country of origin. Instead, they were camped in the refugee camps in Nepal for over 10 years. While Nepal provided them with temporary refuge, they were ineligible to seek residency/citizenship rights there, remaining confined to the refugee camp area. They often flee from violent and life-threatening conditions that significantly impact their physical and psychosocial health. As a result, their health experiences are not only complex but often undiagnosed. Therefore, it is critical that research and medical health-care systems understand, assess, identify, and implement optimum health care for this underserved global population. However, at present, refugees are underrepresented in research and experience poor quality of care in the medical health-care system.

To better understand and examine refugee health care requires us to shift our perception of the ways in which we define and discuss refugee identities. Research often refers to refugee groups as "hard to reach," but this perception completely negates the hazardous colonial approach of Western cannon research. Underrepresentation of diverse researchers and a lack of cross-cultural understanding of diversity in communities cumulatively validates this misleading narrative of refugee groups being "hard to reach" (Abrams, 2010). The cultural humility lens then becomes crucial in addressing these colonial terminologies and reframing the ways in which we approach refugee health. Cultural humility pushes us to address institutional accountability and fix any power imbalances existing between interacting parties (Tervalon & Garcia, 1998). Fixing power imbalance starts with redefining refugee identities. Addressing institutional accountability starts with centering refugee lived experience as it relates to colonization. Therefore, an active practice of cultural humility with refugees involves reassessing perceptions of refugee identities and redirecting the approach to discussing their lives, issues they face, and the foundations of their status. By doing so, we can reject the notion of refugees being hard to reach and instead focus on the gaps in research, health care, and organizational entities that lack culturally appropriate tools to connect and work with refugee groups. Otherwise, we will continue to observe disparities in refugee health care.

In fact, health-care inequity was a prime driver for the creators of the concept of cultural humility (Tervalon & Garcia, 1998). This inequity is most experienced by racially and ethnically minoritized populations at an intersectional level. Refugees, in particular, are severely impacted by health-care disparities due to their social disposition in the global world. Cultural humility in refugee health is crucial because it requires researchers, health-care providers, and any organizational entities to take accountability for the structural framework that presents a barrier to health care among refugees. My intention with this narrative is to provide a perspective that is central to the refugee experience within U.S. health care. In no way can I claim this narrative to be a generalized perception of *all* refugees. My wish is to provide a deeper understanding of one of their perceptions that will guide us in practicing cultural humility across *all* of our interactions with them. Reflexivity is about acknowledging your role in the research process. With respect to this, I discuss reflexivity as an intentional approach to cultural humility across all human interactions.

MY SOCIAL POSITIONING

My approach to understanding cultural humility in refugee health is from the perspective of a cross-cultural researcher with ethnographic field experience working with refugee communities. As a multilingual and multicultural community member, I value reflexivity in my research and the ways in which my position impacts the individuals and communities that I work with. The stories that I share are a direct reflection of my key takeaways from the field; however, reflexivity is an iterative process. Thus, these lessons from the field are also subject to growth and change. The more we indulge in cultural humility as a reflexive practice to human interaction, the closer we get to our understanding of collective lived experiences. Utilize what feels appropriate to you and reflect on those aspects that could benefit from a deeper examination of cultural humility.

LESSONS FROM THE FIELD

During my time in the field with a group of ethnically Nepali-speaking refugee women and their English as a second language (ESL) teacher, an interesting incident occurred. The teacher asked one of the women to rate their health experience in the refugee camps on a scale of one to ten (one being the worst and ten being the best). Instead of providing a numerical rating, the woman shared a story describing her family's experience when they had to transport her husband to the nearest hospital from their camp location. The teacher kept interrupting and asking her to simply give him a numerical rating, but the woman kept ignoring him and continued with her story. After a few interruptions from the teacher, the woman got frustrated and abruptly gave him a numerical rating of ten, when in fact her story described a horrific experience with the refugee camp's clinic. For me, this incident highlighted one of the first reflections on the need for cultural humility in refugee health research. A huge proportion of resettled refugees in the United States are preliterate without an understanding of research concepts. To them, numerical ratings simply do not hold any value. However, they possess the power of narrative storytelling through which they express and share their experiences of displacement, resettlement, and health care. Their narratives serve as an important source of data when examining refugee health.

Another instance of the power of narrations was reflected during a study where I assessed the role of health-care providers in refugee maternal care. I interviewed medical doctors, certified nurse midwives, and medical interpreters to understand their interactions with refugee women. One of the common themes that emerged from the study was the significance of storytelling as a way of describing refugee women's health issues and their overall health status. As many of you may know, patients are typically required to fill out a health history form when visiting a doctor. Refugee women often use interpreters to assist them with language translation. The interpreters shared that for each question in the health history form that required the women to answer with either a "yes" or "no," they often responded instead with a story. Practitioners also shared the women's "indirect" ways of responding to health questions through storytelling. This is because, for refugee women, their lived experiences are the only documentable forms of their health status. Given that medical care during displacement in refugee camps is infrequent to nonexistent, most refugees do not have well-documented health records to use as reference sources.

Consequently, health-care providers are often challenged with their approach to adequately caring for this population. When refugee stories are overlooked, interrupted, and disregarded, it further strengthens the barriers in communication and relationship building between refugees and organizational entities. In my study, refugee women often described a disconnect between them and the health-care system. As a justifiable consequence of their displacement, they internalized their continued poor health status post-resettlement. This perception only reinforces the power imbalances between refugees and U.S. systemic structures, in which we as individuals and communities participate and perpetuate.

As individuals, researchers, and health-care providers, we must consistently be innovative in our strategies to better understand and examine the health experiences and statuses of refugees. This is where cultural humility becomes essential by allowing flexibility in our approach to data collection that aligns with refugees' understanding of sharing such information. This is foundational to practicing cultural humility in refugee research. Having the patience to listen to refugee storytelling and strategically examining their stories to probe culturally relevant health questions are crucial tools for incorporating cultural humility in refugee caregiving. At a systemic level, inclusivity of refugee voices in the research, health-care, and policy fields assures appropriate representation of their experiences. Above all, humanizing and embracing refugee stories and their lived experiences essentializes our conscious practice of cultural humility toward this group.

Reflexivity serves as one of the foundational practices of cultural humility, particularly when working with refugee populations. Collectively reflecting on our social positions, while actively listening and engaging with refugees, helps to address existing power imbalances and holds colonial frameworks accountable for redefining and recentering the refugee experience. Just as reflexivity has been a crucial praxis to my practice of cultural humility, I encourage you to dive deeper into your own (sub)conscious approaches to understanding refugee health and their experiences.

REFERENCES

Abrams, L. S. (2010). Sampling "hard to reach" populations in qualitative research: The case of incarcerated youth. *Qualitative Social Work, 9*(4), 536–550.

Tervalon, M., & Murray-Garcia, J. (1998). Cultural humility versus cultural competence: a critical distinction in defining physician training outcomes in multicultural education. *Journal of Health Care for the Poor and Underserved, 9*(2).

United National High Commissioner for Refugees (UNHCR) (2019). *Refugee data finder*. UN Refugee Agency. https://www.unhcr.org/refugee-statistics/

16

Indigenous Health and Access

DISMANTLING MEDICAL OPPRESSION THROUGH CULTURAL HUMILITY

Kevin Miller and Celeste Perez

This chapter will explore the complicated history between the U.S. government, tribal sovereignty, and Indigenous health care nationwide. For professionals in any field, understanding the larger context surrounding Indigenous health and access to care is necessary for appreciating the importance of humility, emotional intelligence, and cultural sensitivity. While there are no easy or immediate solutions to the myriad obstacles keeping Indigenous communities from accessible, quality health care, acknowledging such obstacles is the first step toward progress.

THE HISTORY OF THE FEDERAL GOVERNMENT'S RESPONSIBILITY FOR INDIGENOUS HEALTH

The United States has a long-existing duty to provide health care and access to medical services to Indigenous peoples (IP) living within its borders (IHS, 2015). Treaties, Supreme Court jurisprudence, federal legislation, and even language within the Constitution itself have established this duty, and the Department of Health and Human Services houses the Indian Health Service (IHS) to assist in managing this responsibility. Members of over 573 federally recognized tribes and Indigenous populations are eligible for health-care assistance through this program, yet the average life expectancy for IP in the United States is 5.5 years shorter than for other races (IHS, 2019).

Limited funding for the IHS and similar missions, coupled with historic distrust of Western institutions held by many Indigenous communities, has resulted in a dearth of accessible health care and health education for IP. These problems persist despite Congress acknowledging its responsibility for providing access to health care for tribal populations. This responsibility originated from treaties signed by tribes with Great Britain during its colonial expansion into North America. The Snyder Act of 1921 earmarked funding for tribal health care, but in the century since, we have seen these budget appropriations stagnate, shrink, and fail to adequately equip tribal communities with the tools and personnel necessary for whole health services (*The Economist*, 2021).

IMPROVING HEALTH-CARE ACCESS FOR INDIGENOUS PEOPLES

Increasing IHS Funding to Establish Baseline Standards

Cultural humility begins with understanding the background and historical contexts of the patients that practitioners serve. It can start with empowering and incentivizing Indigenous providers financially. Funding for the IHS needs to go beyond the paltry and inadequate budget that leaves IP susceptible to negligent care by overworked and undertrained professionals. Increased funding would help to establish a baseline standard of safety within IHS facilities.

Under current funding, IHS patients receive fewer dollars per capita than health care for incarcerated individuals, veterans, and Medicaid recipients within the United States (Jacobs et al., 2019). By comparison, in 2019, the average spend per person for IHS was $4,078, while 2016 data from the Bureau of Prisons showed an average spend of $8,602 per incarcerated individual (IHS, 2020; Government Accountability Office, 2017). In 2019, the Veterans Administration spent an average of $11,800 per person, while the average Medicaid per person expenditure was $14,173 (Veterans Administration, 2022; Yellen et al., 2022). Compared to IP health-care expenditures for IHS, the United States spends more than double the amount per person for any group it has a health-care fiduciary duty to cover. IHS practitioners cannot begin to focus on improving cultural humility practices with IP when they do not have the means to run health-care facilities throughout the year with the dignity that all people deserve.

Acculturating Western Medicine in the Indigenous Context

While governmental bodies are slow to take action in addressing Indigenous health-care needs, IP from North American tribes are working to pick up the slack. Dr. Michelle Johnson-Jennings, a Choctaw Nation Tribal Member, professor, and director of the division of environmentally based health and land-based healing at the Indigenous Wellness Research Institute, lent her expertise to the United Nations' "We Are Indigenous" program series. She noted,

"Ultimately, it is through linking health care work with the culture, history and stories of the community that researchers and healthcare providers can appropriately move forward, therefore, I work closely with community members, elders, and other knowledge keepers to inform and co-develop approaches and research" (United Nations, n.d.).

Dr. Johnson-Jennings is not alone in this approach. The Cherokee Nation of Oklahoma has invested over $400 million in designing, constructing, and staffing new health-care facilities to better serve its members. This includes construction of a massive outpatient health center, with a design informed by the history and culture of the Cherokee Nation to make Indigenous patients feel comfortable when pursuing health-care services. The Cherokee Nation Outpatient Health Center, at 469,000 square feet and rising four stories, is the largest Indian Health Service joint-venture facility and largest tribal outpatient health facility in the United States. Featuring sweeping curves, mixed tones of wood, and rolling blue accent tile flooring, this facility feels nothing like other facilities in the country. It houses over six hundred pieces of art, including examples of Cherokee paintings, pottery, textiles, and art from other mediums, carefully curated by Director of Cultural Art and Design Gina Olaya. Despite its massive footprint, it is a welcoming, warm facility that is inviting and modern without emulating the cold and sterile feel of other facilities of this size.

While few tribes have resources rivaling those of the Cherokee Nation, this facility is a testament of the ability to balance cultural competency with medical competency. Western facilities do not have to present themselves as free of personality or community in order to appear clean and trustworthy, and perpetuating Cherokee culture and heritage has worked. The Cherokee Nation's health-care facilities saw over 1.3 million patients in Fiscal Year 2020 (Cherokee Nation, 2020). The Cherokee Nation Outpatient Health Center is a beacon of what is possible when Western medicine undergoes acculturation. By filtering Western facilities through an Indigenous lens, the Cherokee Nation was able to develop a truly impressive and state-of-the-art facility that its citizens and members are happy to use.

The norm, if not the expectation, is that acculturation happens the other way around: Indigenous people should and will let go of their own value systems and yield to those of the dominant culture. This norm is responsible for much of the distrust toward Western health care that exists across Indian Country. The United States has taken Indigenous lands and enacted policies aimed at erasing the Indigenous identity entirely. Given this history, it is no surprise that Indigenous health and health care are precipitous, with the patient pool having legitimate concerns that seeking Western treatment means facing certain death.

"'Sickness' is what is happening to the patient. Listen to him. Disease is what is happening to science and to populations." This quote by Dr. Lawrence Weed, first recorded in 1978, describes one of the core obstacles to effective health-care treatment today. Western culture reveres a system of dominance and subservience, and in the health-care context, it means providers who were reared and educated within Western systems struggle to grasp the cultural nuance required to successfully reach and treat Indigenous patients.

Even five decades later, the late Dr. Weed's statement on the distinction between sickness and disease still rings true. It echoes the enduring truth that the most profound impacts of racism manifest as inaction in the face of need. Until the systems that govern Western medicine concede some of the expectations perpetuated by virtue of being Western systems, acculturation can only happen at the expense of marginalized communities whose health is already in jeopardy from the structures in place. Even if it means Western systems must be acculturated through an Indigenous lens, involving Indigenous populations in the development and ongoing operation of the facilities that aim to treat them is not only necessary but a just and fair step that must be taken to right centuries of wrongs.

Empowering and Incentivizing Indigenous Providers

Acculturation is only one step to addressing the inadequate health-care access in Indian Country but an inevitable necessity if equitable health care is to become a true reality. It is also, realistically, the most difficult step. Empowering Indigenous health-care providers, as well as incentivizing both their education and subsequent return to provide care within Indian Country, is also a critical and important step. While this would be easier to achieve following widespread acculturation, the likelihood of voluntary systemic change is so minuscule that empowering and incentivizing Indigenous providers is the more logical and immediate pathway forward.

The 2020 U.S. Census revealed a jump in self-reported Indigenous identity of over 85 percent, with the population of Indigenous people growing from just over five million people to nearly ten million between 2010 and 2020 (Indian Country Today, 2021). It is estimated that 58 percent of IP in the United States are within IHS service boundaries, leaving 42 percent of IP without access to guaranteed health care as promised by the U.S. government (Jacobs et al., 2019). Despite this large demographic growth and presence, as of 2018, fewer than 2,600 physicians of Indigenous heritage (0.3 percent of all physicians) were practicing in the United States as compared to 516,304 white physicians (56.2 percent of all physicians) (AAMC, 2019).

Donald K. Warne, MD, MPH, and associate dean for diversity, equity, and inclusion at the University of North Dakota, attributes this lack of representation, at least in part, to recruitment issues. Non-Indigenous doctors are often reluctant to relocate to rural areas to practice because these areas are often impoverished and lack resources and housing. Dr. Warne notes that "[Indigenous peoples] are more likely to return to our communities." Unfortunately, this lack of resources also puts a strain on the ability of IP to pursue medical school in the first place. Dr. Warne has discussed at length the high dropout rates in Indian Country, noting the Northern Plains rate of over 50 percent: "If less than half of your population graduates from high school, where are the doctors going to come from?" (Robeznieks, 2019).

The University of North Dakota is not unfamiliar with the issue of Indigenous health-care provider scarcity. In 1973, it launched Indians Into Medicine (INMED), a program that has recruited and trained over 250 providers with Indigenous heritage. INMED has expanded over the decades, adding support for physical and occupational therapy training, and its model has been replicated in other programs at the university (Kirk, 2018).

Siobhan Wescott, MD, MPH, is Athabascan from Fairbanks, Alaska, and the former assistant director of INMED. Now the first endowed professor and director of American Indian health at the University of Nebraska's College of Public Health, Dr. Wescott points to census-type data as one of her concerns. She expressed the difficulty in accurately capturing the true picture of Indigenous health-care providers, as the Department of Education will not report racial demographic data if a student reports multiple racial backgrounds. Dr. Wescott notes, "For native med students, there are 1,010 currently in med school. But only 177 of those report being only American Indian/Alaska Native. So, 83% of [Indigenous students] under these requirements are lost entirely, and that affects funding decisions to help support new students" (Cueto, 2022).

Experts like Dr. Wescott and Dr. Warne are not alone in their efforts to incentivize the recruitment of Indigenous providers and create a more inclusive, consultation-based climate for IP health care. In 2022, the Department of Health and Human Services hosted its annual regional tribal consultation series. The Association of American Indian Physicians (AAIP) works to increase the presence of Indigenous patients and providers in health-care determinations (The Office of Tribal Affairs and Strategic Alliances, 2022). They have helped to raise awareness of tribal opportunities for scheduling individual consultations through regional offices, spread the word of written testimony submission deadlines, and ensured that tribes are as informed and empowered as possible through the consultation process.

CONCLUSION

While health care has failed to adequately meet the needs of Indigenous Peoples, there is a clearer view than ever before of what immediate changes can successfully affect systemic change. By supporting and uplifting programs like INMED, centering the Indigenous community in discussions surrounding their own health care, and listening to the concerns raised by experts about existing systems perpetuating Indigenous erasure, the entire health-care landscape will evolve and improve in ways the Western approach has never allowed.

REFERENCES

AAMC. (2019). *Diversity in Medicine: Facts and Figures 2019*. https://www.aamc.org/data-reports/workforce/interactive-data/figure-18-percentage-all-active-physicians-race/ethnicity-2018

Accardi, M.T. (2013). Feminist pedagogy for library instruction. Sacramento, CA: Library Juice Press.

Cherokee Nation. (2020). *Cherokee Nation's popular annual financial report for fiscal year ended September 30, 2020*. https://www.cherokee.org/media/2j0hyety/pafr-fy20-_final.pdf

Cueto, I. (2022, April 5). *"We don't have a say": Siobhan Wescott wants to elevate the voices of Native Americans in public health*. STAT. https://www.statnews.com/2022/04/05/siobhan-wescott-wants-to-elevate-the-voices-of-native-americans-in-public-health/

The Economist. (2021, April 26). How do Native Americans get health care? https://www.economist.com/the-economist-explains/2021/04/26/how-do-native-americans-get-health-care

Government Accountability Office. (2017, July 31). *Bureau of prisons: Better planning and evaluation needed to understand and control rising inmate health care costs*. https://www.gao.gov/products/gao-17-379

IHS. (2015, January). *Basis for health services*. https://www.ihs.gov/newsroom/factsheets/basisforhealthservices/

IHS. (2019, October). *Disparities*. https://www.ihs.gov/newsroom/factsheets/disparities/

IHS. (2020, August). *IHS profile*. https://www.ihs.gov/newsroom/factsheets/ihsprofile/#:~:text=Per%20Capita%20Personal%20Health%20Care,expenditure%20per%20user%20population%3A%20%244%2C078%20;%20https://www.gao.gov/products/gao-17-379

Indian Country Today. (2021, August 13). *2020 Census: Native population increased by 86.5 percent*. https://indiancountrytoday.com/news/2020-census-native-population-increased-by-86-5-percent

Jacobs, B., Gallagher, M., & Heydt, N. (2019). Aging in harmony: Creating culturally appropriate systems of health care for aging American Indian/Alaska Natives. *Journal of Gender, Race and Justice, 22*(1), 1+. https://link.gale.com/apps/doc/A594429790/HRCA?u=nhmccd_main&sid=bookmark-HRCA&xid=fea60563

Kirk, L. (2018). Report of the Council on Medical Education CME Report 5-A-18 Subject: Study of Declining Native American Medical Student Enrollment. A. M. Association. https://www.ama-assn.org/system/files/2021-05/a18-cme-05.pdf

Marcinko, T. (2016). *More Native American doctors needed to reduce health disparities in their communities*. AAMC.org. https://www.aamc.org/news-insights/more-native-american-doctors-needed-reduce-health-disparities-their-communities

Office of Tribal Affairs and Strategic Alliances. (2022, August). *Bi-weekly updates*. https://www.aaip.org/sites/aaip/uploads/documents/OTASA_Updates/OTASA_Bi_Weekly_Updates___August_12_2022.pdf

Robeznieks, A. (2019, August 22). *Native Americans work to grow their own physician workforce*. American Medical Association. https://www.ama-assn.org/delivering-care/health-equity/native-americans-work-grow-their-own-physician-workforce

Smith, M. (2018). Native Americans: A crisis in health equity. *Human Rights, 43*(4). https://www.americanbar.org/groups/crsj/publications/human_rights_magazine_home/the-state-of-healthcare-in-the-united-states/native-american-crisis-in-health-equity/

United Nations. (n.d.). *Indigenous healthcare and revitalization*. https://www.un.org/en/academic-impact/we-are-indigenous-%E2%80%98culture-meets-care%E2%80%99-essential-indigenous-healthcare-and

Veterans Administration. (2022, June 7). *National Center for Veterans Analysis and Statistics*. U.S. Department of Veterans Affairs. https://www.va.gov/vetdata/expenditures.asp

Weed, L. L. (1978). *Your health care and how to manage it*. Rev. ed. Essex Publishing.

Yellen, J., Walsh, M., Becerra, X., & Kijakazi, K. (2022). *2022 annual report of the boards of trustees of the Federal Hospital Insurance and Federal Supplementary Medical Insurance trust funds*. https://www.cms.gov/files/document/2022-medicare-trustees-report.pdf

17

Embracing Cultural Humility to Adjust Teaching and Reference Methods for Graduate Health Sciences Students

Margaret Henderson

POSITIONALITY STATEMENT

I am a cishet white woman who has worked in libraries for over thirty-five years. I have lived through the transition from print card catalogs, indexes, books, and journals to electronic versions. I have worked in hospital, special, and academic libraries. Though I have lived and worked in the United States for over thirty years, I am a Canadian with a Bachelor of Science (BSc) in ecology and evolution and an MLIS from a Canadian university.

BUILDING UP EXPERIENCE

We are all shaped by our experiences. As a teenager, I was a swimming instructor for fearful beginners, which helped me learn compassion for those I was teaching. Studying ecology and evolution gave me a grounding in biological literature and research methods. After getting my BSc degree, I enrolled in library school in the late 1980s. I was prepared for the teaching methods there because my grandmother had attended the same library school. She told me about the utilization of the Socratic method, where students read about different topics and wrote reports prior to class, which were then collected and graded. During the class, the professor would return the papers and facilitate a discussion, prompting specific students to present things from their reports.

This teaching method, now often referred to as the "flipped classroom," serves two purposes: it gets students to learn about a topic in ways beyond just a lecture, and it encourages them to listen to others as they engage in discussion.

Reference services was the class that helped to focus my library career. My section of the class was taught by Catherine S. Ross, notably coauthor of *Conducting the Reference Interview* (2002), along with other books and multiple articles on reference and sense-making research. During the course, we were consistently warned not to jump to conclusions too early but rather encouraged to use active listening skills, focus on the complete story, reflect back the questions, and then provide an answer (Ross & Dewdney, 1989). This advice was extremely helpful when working with medical students doing placements in urban and rural settings where getting the whole picture is critical to finding the best answer. Additionally, as director of research data management, I incorporated a data interview into every project to allow researchers to explain their entire projects before suggestions were offered.

YOU DON'T KNOW WHAT YOU DON'T KNOW

After years of working in biomedical research and hospital libraries, supporting students and researchers in a health sciences library, and establishing research data services at a Carnegie Classification R01 university library, I moved to a border city R02 Hispanic Serving Institute. With over thirty years of experience, I was confident in my ability to be a health sciences librarian. However, my assistance to biomedical researchers, doctors, and students in an East Coast inner city did not fully prepare me to support students and faculty in public health and nursing who were working with communities in the inner city of a large West Coast city along the Mexican border. Also, the research needs of students doing outreach to rural Virginia or the Dominican Republic differ significantly from those working in rural desert areas around the border.

My transition was extreme. Richmond, Virginia, is 44.8 percent white, 45.2 percent Black or African American, and 7.3 percent Hispanic or Latino, which contrasts sharply with San Diego City, California, which is 58.2 percent White, 30.1 percent Hispanic or Latino, and 6.0 percent Black or African American (U.S. Census Bureau, n.d.). As I worked with students and faculty who were developing programs for local communities, I had to consider race and ethnicity as well as urban and rural settings when looking for articles. Admittedly I did not consider right away that my daily consultations with students in nursing, exercise and nutrition sciences, and public health helped me learn more about the specifics of the region. I was impressed by the dedication of the students and their sensitivity to the issues of the communities they were studying. They helped me learn more about what I could do to support their work, including keeping notes about the student topics, allowing me to reflect on new subjects and terminologies.

MAKING THE EFFORT TO LEARN MORE

I had not given much consideration to the teaching theories that could support my instructional methods. I quickly realized there was a wealth of knowledge to explore, and I had much to learn to enhance my pedagogical skills. I attended workshops, read more, and talked with colleagues. I enrolled in a feminist librarianship course and found the aspects of feminist pedagogy as described by Maria Accardi (2010) to be very useful. I discovered that some of the principles had been introduced in health sciences teaching, including collaborative classrooms, student centered activities, flipped classes, team-based learning, and more recently, interdisciplinary teams.

Broadly speaking, feminist pedagogy encourages learners to be open to new perspectives and to have empathy for those viewpoints. Feminist librarianship also plays a role in reference interviews, especially when students have topics with multiple viewpoints. One approach is to actively listen to their thoughts on the topic, then help them find what is needed, with a few suggestions for related viewpoints. When students have broad topics, I sometimes gently suggest narrowing the topic by considering a feminist perspective.

I realize now that cultural humility comes naturally from feminist pedagogy. When you begin to recognize the experiences and viewpoints of women from different races, classes, abilities, or sexualities, it is easy to spread that empathy to everyone. Once you have empathy for everyone, you become more willing to speak up for diverse viewpoints.

Servant leadership is another philosophy I have learned about and incorporated into my work. This concept has the goal of listening to everyone and letting group concerns and ideas inform your work (Janssen, 2018). As I familiarized myself with my new institution and administrative structure, some of the principles of servant leadership, such as listening to others first, advocating for those who are starting out, and stepping back to see the big picture, fit well with the way I was trying to interact with my new community.

The idea of questioning authority, as discussed in Paulo Freire's *Pedagogy of the Oppressed* (2018), is significant in the realm of critical pedagogy as it works well when assisting students who are engaging with marginalized urban and rural communities. On a personal level, it is important not to assume you know more than the person you are helping. Taking a resource-based perspective, I find that, "often, professors and students have to learn to accept different ways of knowing, new epistemologies, in the multicultural setting" (hooks, 1994, 41). Critical pedagogy is useful in public health classes because the relevant evidence won't always be a peer-reviewed trial with lots of participants. It could be a report from a grant recipient who tried a diabetes program in a low-income area of a large city or a program description from a tribal council. Because critical pedagogy includes an antiauthoritarian approach to examining issues, it questions some of the conventional ways information literacy defines authority.

PULLING IT ALL TOGETHER

So how does everything I have read about and practiced align with the principles of cultural humility? Through an interactive process and concept analysis of sixty-two articles on cultural humility, Foronda et al. (2016) identified five attributes of cultural humility that fit well with my readings, experiences, and interactions. Most importantly, being open-minded and receptive to interactions with diverse individuals aligned as an integral part of my work with students.

Self-awareness of one's strengths, limitations, values, biases, and beliefs is often hard to accomplish. However, the diversity, equity, and inclusion courses I have taken have helped to increase my awareness of the biases I bring to my work and interactions and have given me constructive ways to learn more about myself. Egolessness is another attribute that was identified in the concept analysis of cultural humility. Embracing humility so I could learn from the students I was working with was one of the first steps in my journey since I realized I had a lot to learn.

The fourth attribute of cultural humility is supportive interactions. The more I embraced humility and openness, the more positive human exchanges I had with those around me, enabling me to learn more about the needs of the groups I served. The final attribute, self-reflection and critique, is key to ensuring continuous improvement as I learn from my daily encounters. Employee resource groups, also known as affinity groups, might offer another avenue to learn about historically underrepresented and underserved populations on campus, leading to collaborative resources for teaching and research.

PUTTING THE IDEAS TO WORK

As I internalized new ideas, I spent time reflecting on my teaching methods and developing a new class structure. The revamped class started by covering the basics of searching in the library catalog and PubMed, then stressed the idea that depending on the topic there may be limited resources. When looking for evidence to support something like a public health education program, it is important to acknowledge that peer-reviewed literature is not the only source for help. Searching beyond library resources for funder and government reports on programs, and other forms of gray literature, is crucial to success.

Once they had the basics, I gave the students case studies that had a health disparities or multicultural component and encouraged them to search for supporting resources. I used cases from the Western Public Health Casebooks (https://www.schulich.uwo.ca/publichealth/cases/index.html). Using cases and examples that reflect real-world problems is an important component in my classes. The cases covered various underrepresented groups, Indigenous populations, rural maternal health, and programs for drug users.

I provided minimal case information to give the students flexibility in determining their approach to the cases, but there were still challenges in finding relevant peer-reviewed literature. These challenges served as good examples of what students might encounter in the workforce or with academic research.

I was also open to students using their lived experiences as they found resources. For instance, one group investigated the integration of ambulance electronic health record systems (EHR) into hospital EHRs, and a student in the group was actually an emergency responder. In another class, a group looking at maternal care had a student who was looking at that issue in local Hispanic communities. One of my primary objectives for these classes was that there was no right answer. The ability of the students to find and recognize different types of evidence without being overwhelmed was the learning outcome. At the conclusion of the class, students shared their findings and search methodologies, so the whole class could learn new research techniques.

I also brought the new ideas to the research consultations I worked on. I had to explore little-used MeSH terms and learn whole new vocabularies, including terms from "prematoras" to "poppers." I used this newfound knowledge to help develop search strategies for students doing capstone projects, dissertations, or theses on their chosen topics. I was in awe of the students and their commitment to going out into the field to improve the lives of underserved groups. Their dedication not only taught me to be a better searcher but also expanded my view of what students can do in a short-term research project.

Ultimately, I decided to develop a course to teach librarians how to create a team-based, case-based, critical pedagogy library class tailored for their institutions. Due to the impact of COVID-19, I was unable to present the course in person, but I adapted and offered an online version of the course. In this virtual setting, I used the same real-world cases for my examples, emphasizing the importance of seeking diverse sources beyond just peer-reviewed articles. There was an interesting moment at the end of the class when one participant expressed difficulty in doing the exercise, which prompted a group discussion of how hard it was working with real-world cases. I think this is one of the best takeaways when we look at trying to help people who are doing work with underserved groups. Finding evidence is not going to be easy.

CONCLUSION

1. Learn about your institution's student body and/or workforces, as well as the communities and populations they serve.
2. Reflect on your own biases—regularly—and try to adjust.
3. Let go of the idea that you are always the expert—even when working with students.
4. Listen to your students, faculty, fellow employees, and patrons.

5. Do not assume what works in one place, or that what works for you in one class or institution can work in another. Even something as basic as information literacy can be taught with a different context or pedagogy in different places or on different subjects. Go into new situations with a cultural humility mindset, and learn what is best for each new situation.
6. Be kind to yourself. There will always be circumstances where you don't have the time or energy to carefully plan but you end up teaching or answering by habit, and then later you wish you had been more thoughtful. When facing these times, just reflect. As long as you are making the effort to work within a cultural humility framework, you are moving forward.

REFERENCES

Foronda, C., Baptiste, D. L., Reinholdt, M. M., & Ousman, K. (2016). Cultural humility: A concept analysis. *Journal of transcultural nursing: Official Journal of the Transcultural Nursing Society, 27*(3), 210–217. https://doi.org/10.1177/1043659615592677

Freire, P., Ramos, M. B., Macedo, D. P., & Shor, I. (2018). *Pedagogy of the oppressed* (M. B. Ramos, Trans.; 50th anniversary edition). Bloomsbury Academic.

hooks, b. (1994). *Teaching to transgress: Education as the practice of freedom.* Taylor & Francis.

Janssen, D. (2018). *Upside-down leadership: A zoo veterinarian's journey to becoming a servant leader.* San Diego Zoo Global.

Ross, C. S., & Dewdney, P. (1989). *Communicating professionally: A how-to-do-it manual for library applications.* Neal-Schuman.

Ross, C. S., Nilsen, K., & Dewdney, P. (2002). *Conducting the reference interview: A how-to-do-it manual for librarians.* Neal-Schuman.

U.S. Census Bureau. (n.d.). *Quick facts.* U.S. Department of Commerce. https://data.census.gov/

18

Accessibility and Disability

MOVING THROUGH SPACE

Lydia Nadine Collins

This chapter is written from the perspective of a Black, foreign-born, disabled cisgender woman who navigates the world using an assistive device. Throughout my twenty-year career as a library practitioner and program manager, I have embraced cultural humility, "a lifelong process of self-reflection and self-critique whereby the individual not only learns about another's culture, but one starts with an examination of her/his own beliefs and cultural identities" (Tervalon & Murray-Garcia, 1998).

Five years ago, my life and work took a sudden turn when I was diagnosed with a chronic health condition. As a result, I now rely on an assistive device for physical mobility, which makes my disability visible. In this chapter, my goal is to share stories that emphasize the importance of cultural humility and systemic responsiveness for faculty, staff, and students. Understanding this importance requires individuals to actively consider others' perspectives and points of view. It also entails recognizing that being "able-bodied" is a temporary condition, as my personal journey exemplifies.

I hope that individuals who bear witness for colleagues, students, or loved ones with invisible and visible disabilities will find this chapter relevant. My recommendations are intended to guide institutional decision makers in creating inclusive and empowering academic environments for all individuals, regardless of their physical, intellectual, mental, spiritual, or psychological "movement through space."

TERMINOLOGY IMPORTANCE AND IMPLICATIONS

The federal civil rights law, the Americans with Disabilities Act (ADA), established parameters and protocols to protect individuals from discrimination based on disability in various aspects of life, including employment, accessing services and goods, and participation in local and state government programs (U.S. Department of Justice Civil Rights Division n.d.). However, the terms "accessibility" and "disability" often carry negative connotations. According to the Oxford English Dictionary (OED) Online, "accessibility" is defined as "the quality or condition of being accessible (in various senses)," while "disability" is defined as "lack of ability (to discharge any office or function); inability, incapacity; weakness." Often, these preassigned labels are frequently associated with demeaning terms that emphasize limitations. Considering this, I chose to address this topic through a social justice lens. "A social justice approach to disability in higher education means beginning with the assumption that people's abilities and rights to contribute to and benefit from higher education are not dependent on their bodies or psyches conforming to dominant norms" (Evans et al., 2017, xiii).

CULTURAL HUMILITY, ACCESSIBILITY, AND ACADEMIA

Cultural humility and cultural responsiveness urge educators to actively rethink equity in academia. It requires introspection (to recognize one's own tacit assumptions) and outward reflection (to foster an appreciation for the lived experiences of others). Engaging in this compare-and-contrast exercise will generally reveal differences, which serve as the foundation for systemic institutional policies and procedures, specifically addressing visible and invisible disabilities, both temporary and permanent. These measures are designed to ensure comprehensive support for employees and students alike. By suspending one's own comfortable cultural and situational assumptions, colleagues and leaders can recognize the interconnectedness of all members within the academic community in an effort to collectively achieve academic excellence.

Sharing some of my experiences in professional settings since my diagnosis may help to illustrate some of the changes needed. I now rely on a cane for assistance while walking. On multiple occasions, library colleagues and users have gestured toward my cane and asked, "What's wrong with you?" or "What's your cane for?" There have even been comments like, "I hope you can keep up with us here." These interactions stem from the assumption that I am somehow "less than" and incapable of performing the work. However, is this any different than someone wearing glasses or contact lenses to assist with vision, or using a hearing aid for increased auditory perception?

In my experience, there is a generalized insensitivity in the workplace among individuals who do not identify as having a disability, which is compounded by a widespread lack of awareness regarding the harmful impact of careless communication. In one of my professional positions I was required to travel, and I did this for over seven years without complaint or regret. Upon returning to work following a medical leave, I attended a team meeting in a conference room where upcoming travel was being discussed. I volunteered that I had a trip scheduled later that month, but before I could even complete my sentence, a member of the leadership team interrupted me and said, "Well, if you need me to tell them that you're handicapped now and can't travel, I can do that. No one will think differently about you for it."

While the intention behind the comment may have been well-meaning, the use of deficit language was hurtful and reflected ableism, which is "discrimination or prejudice against individuals with disabilities" (Merriam-Webster, n.d.). I was grateful that a colleague immediately spoke up and said "No, that was inappropriate. You just called Lydia handicapped in front of the team. How is that ever OK? It's not." Having this colleague publicly advocate for me and serve as an ally provided me with the strength to respond. I expressed that it was too early for me to determine how I would need to move differently in the workspace; therefore, I would keep the leadership informed about any reasonable accommodations or modifications required to continue performing my job effectively.

As I sat in that room with my team, I knew that the decision-makers now perceived me as both Black and disabled—personal attributes regarded not as valuable but rather as deficiencies. Emphasizing positive concepts of empowerment rather than perpetuating language that suggests deficiency is especially important for a Black woman working in academia. Reflecting later on this event, I mourned the loss of my former "able-bodied" self. However, I also realized that I needed to redefine the concept of "able-body," not only for myself but also for the other 22 percent of the population with disabilities (Sullivan, 2021).

NAVIGATING ACADEMIC WORKPLACES

Academics with disabilities face a variety of challenges when it comes to accessing the tools and resources necessary to fulfill their responsibilities. When I sought accommodations as a staff/faculty member, I was sent to the student services division, only to learn that they did not have a designated position to address such requests. Employees at institutions of higher education who disclose a disability often experience this void. While their disclosure is acknowledged, no systemic institutional policies, procedures, or structures are in place to deliver the assistance needed.

Due to the limited capacity of institutions to support faculty and staff with disabilities, employees must devote considerable time and energy to obtain requisite resources. I recall one extreme (but not atypical) example when I attended an organization-wide training where, several weeks ahead of time, I had requested a "sit to stand" table. However, upon arrival I was instructed to sit in the middle of the room with others in an assigned group, without provision of a sit-stand option. I was concerned about being a distraction to my colleagues while the organizational leadership was unconcerned about my inability to fully participate as a disabled employee, who had explicitly requested reasonable accommodations prior to the event.

Nevertheless, my thoughtful response was to prioritize the experience of the others, thereby demonstrating the essence of cultural humility. Consequently, I never had the opportunity to fully engage in group work during the training. Instead, I remained isolated throughout the entire session because the chairs and tables were placed so closely together that I could not navigate the room with my cane. I recall looking around the room at my (temporarily) able-bodied colleagues and thinking, Not only was I one of few BIPOC employees, but I was also the only person identified as disabled. I felt disrespected and humiliated.

Upon my return to our campus, I requested a meeting with senior leadership to share what had occurred from my perspective. Though an apology was offered for what had transpired, the discussion failed to catalyze any changes in the workplace. This left the burden on me to continue to engage in dialogue about basic access needs. I found myself repeatedly in a vulnerable position, having to educate leaders and advocate for proactive measures to be taken by decision-makers.

On yet another occasion, I experienced the difficulty and humiliation of trying to access restroom facilities due to the absence of clear accessibility policies and procedures. The situation was compounded by unsupportive leadership. When the facility I was in was under construction, the restrooms were closed, requiring employees to use restrooms in another section of the building some distance away. Unfortunately, the automatic door-opening function for handicap accessibility had been deactivated in those restrooms. I promptly notified my immediate supervisor that I was experiencing difficulty accessing restrooms and was instructed to email the library director, which I did with a courtesy copy to my supervisor. The director's response was that I should email the facilities department personnel and include both the library director and my immediate supervisor as courtesy copies on all correspondence.

I cannot overemphasize the feelings of incredible vulnerability and personal exposure that resulted from how this situation was managed—or more accurately, mismanaged. I had to share with people—whom I did not know—that I was physically unable to open the door to get to a bathroom. Before I sent the email, I recall feeling "less than" as I considered canceling my request for the basic human right to use a toilet while at work. I did not want to expose my illness and perceived weakness to yet another set of unfamiliar individuals. I couldn't help but wonder why, after years of excellent service and dedication to my job, my reporting supervisor and library leadership could not take proactive and compassionate action to address a faculty member's need for such a fundamental accommodation as access to restroom facilities.

As I typed the email, I knew that I was no longer considered to be a professional or personal asset to this institution. Since disclosing my illness, I had become a problem, a headache, and an inconvenience. In the end, building personnel claimed that the doors were ADA compliant, having been tested and meeting the legal requirements in terms of weight. It left me wondering, how is it possible that at an institution of higher education, a known and documented issue of restroom access can be dismissed by citing regulatory compliance and refusing to take further action? As a result, I was forced to contact the university's Americans with Disabilities Act (ADA) office to request the director's intervention. Although the ADA officer's scope did not include faculty assistance, the office responded immediately out of a sense of moral responsibility, ensuring that the doors were modified.

CONCLUSION

My generous assumption is that everyone working in academia shares the goal of supporting student success through our diverse contributions. However, given the "busyness" of job duties, there is often little time and attention given to fostering collegial interrelations. Consequently, when chronic or temporary disabilities emerge, inadequate institutional responses complicate and often hinder employee productivity and their ability to contribute effectively. A more holistic appreciation and understanding of the workplace would help us to recognize that we all experience periods of being "dis-abled," whether temporarily or permanently. At the end of the day, the interrelationships among colleagues, including leaders, influence our collective capacity to advance institutional excellence and promote student success.

In an ideal workplace, a new employee would feel confident on day one that coworkers had anticipated basic access requirements for "moving through space," informed by cultural humility philosophy and principles that encourage leaning into basic humanity. Such an approach recognizes that we are all differently abled, with multiple capabilities that evolve with time and practice. Simply put, we all want to be treated like humans. Persons identified as disabled—and oftentimes dismissed—face especially challenging barriers without proactive organizational support systems and associated cultural workplace values to create campus communities of true inclusion.

REFERENCES

Centers for Disease Control and Prevention. (n.d.). *Disability Impacts All of Us* [Infographic]. https://www.cdc.gov/ncbddd/disabilityandhealth/documents/disabilities_impacts_all_of_us.pdf

Evans, N. J., Broido, E. M., Brown, K. R., Wilke, A. K., & Herriott, T. K. (2017). *Disability in higher education: A social justice approach* [e-book edition]. John Wiley & Sons, Incorporated.

Merriam-Webster. (n.d.). *Ableism*. https://www.merriam-webster.com/dictionary/ableism

National Center for Educational Statistics. (n.d.). *Race/ethnicity of college faculty*. Institute of Education Sciences. https://nces.ed.gov/fastfacts/display.asp?id=61

Oxford English Dictionary. (n.d.). *Accessibility*. https://www.oed.com/search/dictionary/?scope=Entries&q=accessibility

Oxford English Dictionary. (n.d.). *Disability*. https://www.oed.com/search/dictionary/?scope=Entries&q=Disability

Sullivan, M. (2021, October 25). *POV: Higher ed institutions would benefit from hiring more faculty and staff with disabilities*. BU Today. https://www.bu.edu/articles/2021/higher-ed-institutions-hiring-more-faculty-staff-with-disabilities/

Tervalon, M., & Murray-Garcia, J. (1998). Cultural humility versus cultural competence: A critical distinction in defining physician training outcomes in multicultural education. *Journal of Health Care for the Poor and Underserved, 9*(2),117–125. https://doi.org/10.1353/hpu.2010.0233

U.S. Department of Justice Civil Rights Division (n.d.). Introduction to the Americans with Disabilities Act. https://www.ada.gov/topics/intro-to-ada/

Index

academia/academic, 6, 34, 48, 74, 103-104, 106, 109, 129, 142-143, 165-169
access to care, 5, 20, 30-31, 33, 131-132, 151-155
accessibility, 165-170
affinity groups, 43, 77, 107-108, 134, 162
    See also employee resource groups
African American Medical Librarians Alliance (caucus), 77
Americans with Disabilities Act (ADA), 166, 169
American Library Association (ALA), 6, 32, 41, 43, 47-48, 78, 103, 109, 115
Association of Research Libraries (ARL), 6, 115
authenticity, 44, 48-49, 74, 81, 87
    deauthenication, 74-75, 79

bias, 5, 25, 31-32, 35, 42-43, 47, 59, 91, 94-95, 99, 106-107
BIPOC, 43, 48, 79, 118, 168
Black (African/American)
    librarians/librarianship, 46-47, 57, 61, 79, 92, 121-128
    (male), 165
    women, 74-75, 109, 165
    library workers, 77
Black Caucus of the American Library Association, 78
building connections, 71-84

cisnormativity, 141

collections development, 34, 45, 107, 129, 139, 142
critical consciousness, 5, 14, 17
critical/cruicial conversations, 76-79, 95-97
critical pedagogy, *See pedagogy*
critical reflection, 47-49, 94
cross-cultural relationships, 79-83
cultural awareness, 12, 42
cultural competence, 3-6, 43, 62, 104, 135-136, 153
    limits, 104
cultural humility,
    characteristics, 82
    definition, 41-42
    health care, 19-25
    historical perspective, 3-8
    homophobia, 123
    intrapersonal, interpersonal, collective (system), 42-46, 98
    mental health, 123
cultural identity, 32, 52-53, 85, 165
cultural knowledge, 4-5 9, 32, 141

dental curricula, 61-67
disability,
    See accessibility
diversity, 66-67, 87, 91, 104
    health professional training programs, 61
    US Census projections, 87

emotional intelligence, 73, 76, 151
employee resource groups, 77, 83, 107-108, 110, 162
    See also affinity groups

gender, 54-55, 92, 107, 123, 141-145

health care, 19-25
    Indigenous, 151-155
    refugee, 147-150
health-care providers/professionals, 19, 21-23, 26, 31-32
health disparities, 25-26, 32, 129, 136, 148
health equity, 20, 32, 35
health literacy, 29-35
Historical Black Colleges & Universities (HBCU), 118, 122
    dental program, 65

identity/identities, 54-60, 79, 80, 91-92, 105, 107
identity groups, 43, 53, 56
    See also affinity groups, employee resource groups
Implicit Association Test, 42, 95, 106
Indigenous/Native health, 151-155
instruction, 62-67
    See also teaching
intercultural communication, 79
intersectionality, 91-93, 99, 105, 107, 133, 135, 137-138, 139

leadership, 85-86, 89-90, 95, 99
LGBTQIA+, 129-140, 142-144
lifelong learning, 15, 31, 72, 81, 91, 103, 105

marginalized, 48-49, 56, 65, 77, 86, 93, 94, 97, 105-106, 115-118, 154, 161
Medical Library Association (MLA), 43, 130, 132
mental health, 122-123, 126-127
microaggressions, 48, 74, 78, 104, 133

National Library of Medicine (NLM), 33
Network of the National Library of Medicine (NNLM), 32-33, 132

nonbinary, 55, 141-143

Obama, Barack, 86

patient care, 20, 62
patient navigators, 34
pedagogy, 17, 36, 156, 161-164
population, U.S., 64, 87
power, 21
privilege, 14, 31, 42, 92-94, 106-107, 115-118
professional development, 63, 103-109
public libraries, 29, 32-33, 44

queer, 92, 129, 133, 135, 137, 143-144

racism, xi, 10, 12, 31, 58, 64-65, 86, 89, 105, 118, 125-126, 154
reference, 132, 160-161
reflexivity, 98, 148, 150
refugee health, 147-150
resettlement, 147, 149
restrooms, 135, 168

self-examination, 5, 71-72
self-reflection, 5, 9, 13, 25, 30-31, 41-42, 45, 80-81, 85, 99, 103, 105-106, 136, 165
servant leadership, 161
Social Identity Theory, 57
social justice, 13, 46, 49, 62, 116, 166
systemic racism, xiii, 3, 122
stereotypes, 32, 57, 94, 106, 121

teaching, 22, 44, 63-63, 98, 159-162, 164
trans inclusivity, 141
transcultural care, 20
transgender, 55, 129-130, 132, 141-143
Trump, Donald, 86

white supremacy culture, 78, 81
whiteness, 79, 104, 115

About the Editors

Shannon D. Jones *(she/her)* is director of libraries for the Medical University of South Carolina in Charleston. Shannon is also director for Region 2 of the Network of the National Library of Medicine, headquartered at MUSC. Before she arrived at MUSC, Shannon worked as associate director for research and education for Tompkins-McCaw Library for the Health Sciences at Virginia Commonwealth University in Richmond. Shannon focuses her research on staff recruitment and retention, diversity, equity, inclusion and belonging in libraries, and leadership in academic health sciences libraries. In 2018, Shannon cofounded the MLA Reads Virtual Book Discussion Club to provide a forum where participants can learn, discuss, and process the implications of a variety of DEI topics in their work as information professionals and in their personal lives. Shannon is coeditor of *Diversity and Inclusion in Libraries: A Call to Action and Strategies for Success*. Her educational background includes an EdD in educational leadership from Charleston Southern University, an MEd in adult learning with a concentration in human resources development from Virginia Commonwealth University, and a master's in library science from North Carolina Central University.

Beverly Murphy *(she/her)* is assistant director for communications and web content management at the Duke University Medical Center Library and Archives. She is also hospital nursing liaison for the Duke Health System and liaison for the students and faculty at the Watts College of Nursing. Beverly has been a librarian for forty-three years and is an alumnus of North Carolina Central University in Durham, North Carolina, where she received a BS in biology and a master's in library science. She is a distinguished member of the Academy of Health Information Professionals and has served in a variety of capacities for the Medical Library Association (MLA), including as the first African American president and the recipient of the Marcia C. Noyes Award, MLA's highest professional distinction. Beverly is an MLA fellow, has served as editor of the *MLA News*, and is a member of the *Journal of the Medical Library Association* (JMLA) editorial board. She is coeditor of *Diversity and Inclusion in Libraries: A Call to Action and Strategies for Success*. Her research interests include librarian core competencies; diversity, equity, inclusion, and belonging; health literacy; library administration; and leadership and management.

About the Contributors

Erica Brody
Research and Education Librarian, Liaison to the School of Dentistry
Assistant Professor
Health Sciences Library, Research and Education
VCU Libraries
Virginia Commonwealth University
ebrody@vcu.edu

Lydia Nadine Collins (she/her)
PhD Student
Department of Transformative Social Change
Saybrook University
lcollins1@saybrook.edu

Nicole A. Cooke, PhD, MEd, MLS (she/her/hers)
Augusta Baker Endowed Chair and Associate Professor
School of Information Science, UofSC
ncooke@mailbox.sc.edu / @BakerChair

Gina R. Costello
Associate Dean
Louisiana State University Libraries
gcoste1@lsu.edu

Kunga Denzongpa, PhD, MPH
Data and Evaluation Manager
Community-Campus Partnerships for Health
kungadenzongpa@gmail.com

Kenny Garcia (he/him/his)
Research and Instruction Librarian
California State University—Monterey Bay
Tanimura & Antle Family Memorial Library
kengarcia@csumb.edu

Xan Y. Goodman (she/her/hers)
    Health Sciences Librarian and Associate Professor University of Nevada, Las Vegas
    xan.goodman@unlv.edu

Andrea Hayes
    Assistant Professor
    Health and Critical Information Literacy Librarian
    Purdue University Libraries and School of Information Studies
    West Lafayette, IN
    hayes261@purdue.edu

Tish Hayes, MLIS, MEd (she/her)
    Information Literacy Librarian
    Moraine Valley Community College Library
    hayesl45@morainevalley.edu

Margaret Henderson, MLIS, AHIP
    Associate Professor Health Sciences Librarian
    San Diego State University
    margaret.henderson@sdsu.edu

Renee F. Hill, PhD, MLIS
    Principal Lecturer, Diversity and Inclusion Officer, Equity Administrator
    University of Maryland
    rfhill@umd.edu

Twanna Hodge, MLIS (she/her/hers)
    PhD Student
    College of Information Studies
    University of Maryland, College Park
    tkhodge20@gmail.com

David G. Keddle (he/him/his)
    Manager, Medical Library Services
    Kaiser Permanente Medical Center
    david.g.keddle@kp.org

Jacqueline Leskovec, MLIS, MA, RN (she/her)
    Network Coordinator
    Network of the National Library of Medicine (NNLM)
    Region 6
    University of Iowa

Hardin Library for the Health Sciences
jacqueline-leskovec@uiowa.edu

Brenda M. Linares, MLIS, MBA, AHIP (she, ella)
Associate Dean of Library Services
University Libraries
University of Missouri–Kansas City
blinares@umkc.edu

Irene M. Lubker, PHD, MLS, MPH, RD, AHIP
Research and Education Informationist
Medical University of South Carolina Libraries
lubker@musc.edu

Kevin Miller
Faculty Fellow, American Indian Law Program
University of Colorado School of Law
kemi6099@colorado.edu

Jane Morgan-Daniel, MLIS, MA (she/her)
Community Engagement and Health Literacy Liaison Librarian
Health Science Center Libraries
University of Florida
morgandanie.jane@ufl.edu

Joni Nelson, PhD, MS
Associate Professor and Director of the Division of Population Oral Health
Medical University of South Carolina James B. Edwards College of Dental Medicine
nelsonjd@musc.edu

Tamara M. Nelson, MLIS, EdS, AHIP
User Services Coordinator
Senior Research and Learning Services Librarian
Associate Professor
The University of Tennessee Health Science Center
Health Sciences Library
tnelso24@uthsc.edu

Conrad Pegues
Assistant Professor
Public Services Librarian
Paul Meek Library

The University of Tennessee at Martin
cpegues@utm.edu

Celeste Perez (she/her/they)
Reference Librarian
Lone Star College CyFair
Celeste.Perez@lonestar.edu

Kammi Y. Sayaseng, DNP, RN, PNP-BC, IBCLC
Associate Professor and Graduate Program Coordinator
Pediatric Nurse Practitioner
California State University, Fresno
School of Nursing
ksayaseng@csufresno.edu

Hannah M. Schilperoort, MLIS, MA (she/her)
Associate University Librarian
Head, Wilson Dental Library
USC Libraries
University of Southern California
schilper@usc.edu

Meredith Solomon, MLS (she/her)
Senior Outreach Officer
Harvard Medical School
Countway Library, Outreach Department
meredith_solomon@hms.harvard.edu

Brandi Tuttle, MSLIS (she/her)
Research and Education Librarian
Duke University Medical Center Library and Archives
brandi.tuttle@duke.edu

Emily Vardell, PhD (she/her)
Assistant Professor
School of Library and Information Management
Emporia State University
evardell@emporia.edu

Teresa Wagner, DrPH, MS, CPH, RD/LD, CPPS, CHWI, DipACLM, CHWC
Assistant Professor, Department of Lifestyle Health Sciences
University of North Texas Health Science Center, School of Health Professions

Clinical Executive for Health Literacy, SaferCare Texas
Fellow and Project Director, Texas Center for Health Disparities
Teresa.Wagner@UNTHSC.EDU

Travis L. Wagner, PhD
Lecturer
College of Information Studies
University of Maryland
twagner@umd.edu

Stacey E. Wahl, PhD
Senior Instructional Design Specialist
Assistant Professor
VCU School of Medicine
Virginia Commonwealth University
stacey.wahl@vcuhealth.org

Rachel Walden, MLIS (she, her, Ms.)
Associate Dean, Professor, Director of the ETSU Medical Library
Medical Library, Biomedical Communications, and Information Technology
Quillen College of Medicine
East Tennessee State University
WALDENRR@mail.etsu.edu

www.ingramcontent.com/pod-product-compliance
Lightning Source LLC
Chambersburg PA
CBHW022013300426
44117CB00005B/167